UNIVERSITY OF MAINE
AT AUGUSTA

AUGUSTA, MAINE

THE POLITICS
OF MOTION

THOMAS A. SPRAGENS, Jr.

THE POLITICS
OF MOTION

The World of
THOMAS HOBBES

WITH A FOREWORD BY
ANTONY FLEW

CROOM HELM LONDON

FIRST PUBLISHED 1973
COPYRIGHT © 1973 UNIVERSITY OF KENTUCKY PRESS
FOREWORD COPYRIGHT © 1973 CROOM HELM LTD.

CROOM HELM LTD
2-10 ST JOHNS ROAD LONDON SW11

ISBN 0-85664-047-6

PRINTED IN GREAT BRITAIN
BY EBENEZER BAYLIS AND SON LTD
THE TRINITY PRESS, WORCESTER, AND LONDON
BOUND BY G. AND J. KITCAT LTD, LONDON

Contents

Contents

Preface

Outrageous in places, astonishingly penetrating in others, the profound and sweeping view of politics which Thomas Hobbes articulated to his scandalized seventeenth-century contemporaries provides perennial fascination for political theorists. And deservedly so. Hobbes was perhaps the greatest political philosopher to write in the English language. He also happened to write at the time of the intellectual revolution which produced our modern Western world. We, therefore, stand to learn much from him—about politics and about ourselves—even if we find his prescriptions ultimately unpalatable.

In this book, I have tried to shed some added light on two principal issues in the ongoing dialogue about Hobbes. First, I hope to contribute to the understanding of the relationship between Hobbes's natural philosophy and his civil philosophy. I argue that Hobbes's political ideas were in fact significantly influenced by his cosmological perceptions, although they were not, and could not have been, completely derived from that source. I also suggest that this influence of Hobbes's conception of 'nature' on his view of politics was accomplished largely by means of analogical permeation. That is, conceptual patterns and models developed to deal with natural phenomena became prisms through which he perceived human and political phenomena. The intellectual dynamics involved, I contend, were essentially those which Thomas Kuhn has described in his discussion of the functions of 'exemplar paradigms'.

The second central theme of this study is the relationship between Hobbes and the Aristotelian world view which constituted the philosophical orthodoxy he rejected. Although many scattered comments on this question may be found in writings on Hobbes, no one seems to have fully recognized the highly structured nature of the relationship between Hobbes

7

and Aristotle. Hobbes, in fact, I argue, undertook a highly systematic transformation of Aristotelian cosmology. There is method and logic both in what he adopted from Aristotle and what he jettisoned. He borrowed the form of the Aristotelian cosmology, but radically refashioned its substance to accommodate the discoveries of contemporaries such as Galileo. Therefore, Hobbes's idea patterns paralleled those of Aristotle to an astonishing degree even as he drastically refashioned their contents.

These two themes, moreover, interact and overlap. The Aristotelian world was a highly coherent one. Perceptions of political events and of natural events were tied together by concepts which were believed applicable to them both. Hobbes saw politics in light of his theory of nature, I argue, partly because the intellectual world he created replicated the homogeneity of the Aristotelian universe.

Because these central themes lie at the heart of the intellectual task which Hobbes set for himself, the logic of exposition which follows approximates very closely, I feel, the 'logic-in-use' which Hobbes himself employed. Therefore, I hope that my argument will be helpful to the relative newcomer to Hobbes, as well as to those who have a fuller familiarity with his thought.

Many of my teachers, colleagues, and students have contributed to the growth of the ideas presented here. I would particularly like to acknowledge my debt to John H. Hallowell, who thoughtfully supervised and contributed to my first systematic explorations into Hobbes, to William H. Poteat, whose insights into the intellectual forces at work in the seventeenth century have been most helpful to me, and to Norman O. Brown, who first introduced me to Hobbes during my undergraduate days at Wesleyan. None of them should be burdened with the responsibility for any of my intellectual sins, but each contributed in his own distinctive way to this work.

I would also like to thank the Duke University Research Council for financial assistance in preparing the manuscript for publication and Professor Antony Flew who has contributed a stimulating introduction.

Mrs. L. F. Hall, Mrs. Judy Baldwin, and Mrs. Doris Ralston provided invaluable assistance in the typing and preparation of the manuscript. David Nordquest helped with the tedious task of proof reading. To them I am grateful also.

Finally, I would like to thank my wife, Ann. Her contributions have been of a different, and more important, order.

Foreword

What surely was and still remains the best critical presentation of the whole Hobbes was first published by Richard Peters in 1956.[1] This seems to have been the first book-length contribution to Hobbes studies in English since that of John Laird twenty-two years earlier.[2] But in the seventeen years since 1956 a further nine books have appeared dealing with, or purporting to deal with, particular aspects of the thought and influence of Hobbes: eight by single authors, and one a collection of papers from various hands.[3] We need, therefore, some very good reason for the adding of yet another volume.

Dr. Spragens can give two, and both can be developed from very characteristic texts in Hobbes. The first comes from Chapter XLVI of *Leviathan*, in the still too rarely appreciated Part IV 'Of the Kingdom of Darkness'. Hobbes writes: 'To conclude, there is nothing so absurd that the old philosophers (as Cicero saith, who was one of them) have not some of them maintained. And I believe that scarce anything can be more absurdly said in natural philosophy, than that which is now called Aristotle's *Metaphysics*; nor more repugnant to government, than much of that he hath said in his *Politics*; nor more ignorantly, than a great part of his *Ethics*.'

This is fine swinging stuff, the protest of a self-consciously anti-Aristotelian intellectual revolutionary. There is plenty more. Two paragraphs later Hobbes begins 'to descend to the particular tenets of vain philosophy, derived to the universities, and thence into the Church, partly from Aristotle, partly from blindness of understanding . . .'. A little later again, still in the same chapter, Hobbes asks: 'But to what purpose (may some man say) is such subtlety in a work of this nature, where I pretend to nothing but what is necessary to the doctrine of government and obedience? It is to this purpose, that men may no longer suffer themselves to be abused by them, that by this doctrine of separated essences, built on the vain philosophy of Aristotle, would fright them from obeying the laws of their country, with empty names; as men fright birds from the corn with an empty doublet, a hat, and a crooked stick. For it is upon this ground that when a man is dead and buried they say his soul (that is his life) can walk separated from his body, and is seen by night among the graves.'

Confronted by vehement, total, and systematic rejections of this sort the wise historian seeks also for the continuities latent beneath the brouhaha of strenuous and ostentatious change. Thus Alexis de Tocqueville looks behind the superficially total transformation wrought by the great French Revolution of 1789, and is then able to discover in the subsequent new order the intensification and fulfilment of many of the most characteristic tendencies of *l'ancien regime*. Similarly in our own time the student of Lenin's anti-liberal socialist revolution of October 1917, if he widens and deepens his historical perspective, can see under the collective autocracy of 'the new Tsars' parallel intensifications and fulfilments of many of the most characteristic policies and ambitions of the old Imperial Great Russia of the Romanovs.

This is what Dr. Spragens, as a wise historian of ideas, has done with the much trumpeted Hobbist rejection of the old established Aristotelian orthodoxy. Of course he finds that Hobbes did make very substantial changes: the revolution was no fraudulent intellectual non-event. But these very substantial changes were changes within a general framework which remained, though certainly not Aristotle's, to a significant extent Aristotelian nevertheless. Others before Dr. Spragens have, as he himself is rightly the first to insist, emphasized the influence of Aristotle upon particular parts of the work of Hobbes. Thus Dr. Spragens quotes Leo Strauss: 'The central chapters of Hobbes's anthropology, those chapters on which, more than anything else he wrote, his fame as a stylist and one who knows men rests for all time, betray in style and contents that the author was a zealous reader, not to say a disciple, of the *Rhetoric*.' But what Dr. Spragens has done is to examine systematically and thoroughly the ways in which Hobbes transformed, while yet in some sense still retaining, an Aristotelian framework.

The treatment by Hobbes of body and soul can serve as a small yet important appetizer. For earlier in that same Part IV of *Leviathan*, in which he was to denounce this dangerous 'doctrine of separated essences, built on the vain philosophy of Aristotle', Hobbes wrote: 'The soul in Scripture signifieth always either the life or the living creature; and the body and soul jointly, the body alive' (Chapter XLIV). What is this if not a view of the nature of man which may be Biblical, but which is certainly Aristotelian also; and which is most emphatically not either Platonic or Cartesian? It was, after all, Aquinas and not the master Aristotle himself who argued that the soul as the form of the body must be a subsistent thing: something, that is, which—unlike a harmony, or a grin, or a temper—could significantly be said to exist separately and in its own right.[4]

The text for the second lesson comes from the Epistle Dedicatory to the *de Corpore*. Hobbes wrote: 'Galileus in our time . . . was the first that opened to us the gate of natural philosophy universal, which is the knowledge of the nature of motion . . . Lastly, the science of man's body, the most profitable part of natural science, was first discovered with admirable sagacity by our countryman Doctor Harvey. Natural philosophy is therefore but young; but civil philosophy is yet much younger, as being no older (I say it provoked, and that my detractors may know how little they have wrought upon me) than my own book *de Cive*.'

The lesson is that Hobbes intended his 'civil philosophy' to be, and believed that it was, a contribution to natural science: a contribution strictly on all fours with the great work of Galileo, and perhaps especially with 'the most profitable' discoveries of 'our countryman Doctor Harvey'. As an aspirant science of the state it begins with what purports to be an appropriately mechanical account of human psychology, centered upon one most fundamental supposed law of tendency: 'For every man is desirous of what is good for him, and shuns what is evil, but chiefly the chiefest of natural evils, which is death; and this he doth by a certain impulsion of nature, no less than that whereby a stone moves downward.'[5]

It is this fundamental putative scientific law of human nature —the law of self-preservation, as we might say—which guarantees that the Hobbist science of the state cannot but be beneficially applied if once it is understood and accepted. It is not, I think, as Dr. Spragens at one point suggests, that 'The ethical tension between "ought" and "is" is grounded in the ontological tension between essence and existence; and if the latter is dissolved, then the former falls apart as well' (page IV-15:098). It is rather—or perhaps this is only a very different way of saying the same thing—that, since people by the fundamental law of their being cannot help doing what in a cool hour they believe will make for their own preservation, they cannot but apply the knowledge which Hobbes offers of how a functioning fully sovereign state is the necessary means to that end.

Hobbes had the very best of reasons for saying in his 'Conclusion' to *Leviathan*: 'Therefore I think it may be profitably printed, and more profitably taught in universities . . . For seeing that the universities are the fountains of civil and moral doctrine, from whence the preachers, and the gentry, drawing such water as they find, use it to sprinkle the same (froth from the pulpit and in their conversation) upon the people . . . by that means the most men . . . will be less likely to serve the ambition of a few discontented persons, in their purposes against the state; and be the less grieved with the contributions necessary for their peace, and defence; and the governors themselves have less cause to maintain at the common charge any greater army than is necessary to make good the public liberty against the invasions and encroachments of foreign enemies.'

To all this it is relevant, but by no means sufficient, to reply that the law of self-preservation, construed thus as a descriptive psychological law, is in fact not true. It is indeed precisely because it just is not in fact true that those who ran away from some mortal danger, when others did not, are apt to appeal as an excuse to this same supposed law—construed equivocally as both descriptive and prescriptive. And it was also, surely, partly because they constituted recalcitrant and intractable falsifying instances against this cherished theoretical fundamental that Hobbes was so incensed by those who insisted upon cooly risking and accepting martyrdom for their religious or political convictions.

In stressing the scientific aspirations of the 'civil philosophy' of Hobbes Dr. Spragens has, of course, again had predecessors.[6] But the message has still not been received and acted upon. There is, therefore, need and room for another attempt to get teachers of political theory to see that it will not do to present Hobbes, Locke, and Rousseau as the famous three, without labouring to show how very different were the ambitions of Hobbes from those of the authors of the *Two Treatises of Civil Government* and of *The Social Contract*.

In this present case the dykes of prejudice which have to be broken down are perhaps more formidable than those thrown up by traditional syllabus divisions within what is allowed to be one subject. Convenient tradition, for example, groups Locke, Berkeley, and Hume as the blessed trinity of British Empiricism; and this has in the past surely misled most of the teachers as well as the taught to assume that Berkeley loomed as large for Hume as he does for us. But in trying to get Hobbes recognized as the would-be William Harvey of the anatomy of the state, we are trying to bridge the deepest chasm in British education. This is a chasm so profound and so much taken for granted that when Sir Charles Snow coined the phrase 'the two cultures' as a label for some of its effects, he and almost all his British readers parochially assumed that what he was thus indicating must be a global phenomenon of our time rather than something produced, or at any rate enormously intensified, by certain almost unique peculiarities of British education in the last hundred years or so.

Hobbes, like Hume a century later, had never heard of 'the two cultures'; and neither knew that there comes a time when all must choose — and the brighter the younger — whether to go onto the arts side or the science side. So neither was aware that *Leviathan* and the *Treatise* were classics, respectively, of political thought and of philosophy; and must as such be, and have been intended to be, contributions not to science but to the humanities. It will take a bulldozer to level the mound of misunderstanding in those who, unlike Hume and Hobbes, find this obvious. More power to Dr. Spragens' motor.

Antony Flew

NOTES

1. *Hobbes* (Harmondsworth and Baltimore: Penguin, 1956. Second edition 1967).
2. *Hobbes* (London: Ernest Benn, 1934).
3. See Note 4 to the Introduction, below.
4. For backing for these claims see: either my article on 'Immortality' in Paul Edwards (Ed.) *Encyclopaedia of Philosophy*; or my *Body Mind and Death* (New York: Collier-MacMillan, 1964); or my *An Introduction to Western Philosophy* (London and Indianapolis: Thames and Hudson, and Bobbs-Merrill, 1971), Chapter IV.
5. *English Works* II, p. 8.
6. The fullest previous development of this aspect is to be found in J. W. N. Watkins *Hobbes's System of Ideas* (London: Hutchinson, 1965). But compare also Richard Peters *Loc. Cit.* and the article 'Hobbes' in D. J. O'Connor (Ed.) *A Critical History of Western Philosophy* (New York and London: Free Press, and Allen and Unwin, 1964).

1

Hobbes the Philosopher

Political theory should not be an antiquarian exercise. Its proper task is the clarification of patterns of political order — those patterns which we inhabit and those for which we should strive. Perhaps unfortunately, however, it does not follow that we are permitted to ignore or to forget our past. Whether it be regarded as an incubus or as a treasure-house, whether we agree with Marx or with Burke, we must recognize that we are inescapably history-laden creatures. As political animals we do not enter upon an empty stage; as political theorists we cannot begin writing upon a clean slate.

Thoughtful students of the political tradition of the West have generally agreed that the ideas of that remarkable seventeenth-century English iconoclast, Thomas Hobbes, comprise one of the most important strands of that tradition. Michael Oake-shott has written: 'The *Leviathan* is the greatest, perhaps the sole, masterpiece of political philosophy written in the English language. And the history of our civilization can provide only a few works of similar scope and achievement to set beside it.'[1] And Leo Strauss has concurred: 'Hobbes's political philosophy is of supreme importance not only for political philosophy as such, i.e. for one branch of knowledge among others, but for modern philosophy altogether, if the discussion and elucidation of the ideal of life is indeed the primary and decisive task of philosophy.'[2] Moreover, this widespread recognition of the significance of Hobbes's thought has tended to increase rather than to abate in recent years. The years since the Second World War have, as Keith Brown recently observed, 'seen a remarkable increase of interest in the writing of Thomas Hobbes.'[3]

B

Since Howard Warrender published his significant study of Hobbes's theory of obligation in 1957, at least seven book-length treatments of Hobbes's thought have appeared.[4]

Several probable reasons for this notable level of contemporary interest in Hobbes's thought are worthy of mention, wholly apart from the more fortuitous and technical academic reasons. The first of these is quite simply the depth and profundity of Hobbes's ideas. While he was sometimes erratic and sporadic in his speculations, his thoughts consistently reach the most fundamental problems of political life; and they do so within the setting of a wide-ranging and largely coherent view of the universe. Any system of ideas with these virtues possesses a kind of perennial relevance which makes recurrent renewals of interest in them a predictable pattern rather than a cause for bemusement.

Another reason for recurrent interest in Hobbes is the recognition that he anticipated some very contemporary problems, methods, and descriptive models in his work. For example, Hobbes's discussions of psychology possess some interesting similarities to comparable discussions in the literature of psychological behaviorism.[5] Some of Hobbes's theories about the nature and status of law are very close to the theories of recent legal positivism. And others have remarked upon the similarities of some of Hobbes's comments about language to the concerns and methods of contemporary linguistic analysis.[6]

Hobbes especially seems modern in his disillusionment with the possibilities of politics and with the instincts of man. Although new currents of ideological utopianism seem to be arising, the dominant tendency of the contemporary Western intellectual world has been toward a sober modesty in its expectations from political man. The early Enlightenment faith in the inexorable progress of the human race to ever greater heights of order, happiness, and liberty survived into the bland optimism of Victorianism; but this optimism has now pretty well disappeared under the onslaught both of harsh political events and of incisive intellectual attacks. The brutalities and absurdities of two world wars dispelled any illusions about the inevitability or the easy attainability of 'peace in our time'. The early bright hopes of some of the Western intelligentsia for communism as an inevitable solution to man's inhumanity to man largely dissipated when the brave and hopeful words of Marx degenerated into the drab and stultifying reality of Stalin. In an age where the somber voices of our tradition, once a distinct minority, are now being heard with attentiveness, Hobbes seems peculiarly appropriate. Like Pascal, Kierkegaard, and Freud, he represents a genuine part of our intellectual tradition which warns us not to confuse our ideals with reality.

The link between the dispelled illusions of the mid-twentieth century and the renewed interest in Hobbes is perhaps best captured in the words of R. G. Collingwood, who wrote in 1942:

> It is only now, towards the middle of the twentieth century, that men here and there are for the first time becoming able to appreciate Hobbes's *Leviathan* at its true worth, as the world's greatest store of political wisdom. . . .
>
> The wars of the present century have taught some of us that there was more in Hobbes than we had supposed. They have taught us that, to see political life as it really is, we must blow away the mists of sentimentalism which have concealed its features from us since the beginning of the eighteenth century. I believe that I am not reporting my own experience alone when I say that the dispelling of these mists by the almost incessant tempest through which we have precariously lived for close on thirty years has revealed Hobbes's *Leviathan* as a work of gigantic stature, incredibly overtopping all its successors in political theory from that day to this.[7]

If Hobbes can speak to us across the span of centuries with meaning and force as, in some ways, a fellow modern man, this ability is more than fortuitous. He lived at a crucial turning point in the intellectual history of the West, what has been termed the 'intellectual revolution of the seventeenth century' or the 'scientific revolution'; and perhaps more than any of his contemporaries he apprehended the truly radical transformation that had taken place. While Descartes was leaving mind and God prophylactically protected from his critical doubt, and while Locke was pouring much old wine into new wineskins, Hobbes's relentless mind insisted upon following out the implications of the new sensibility to the whole span of reality. With this rigorous insistence, Hobbes moved in some areas almost instantaneously to conclusions and images which the mainstream of Western thought reached only step by step, if at all.

Although many new ideas and discoveries have intervened between Hobbes's day and ours, we are nevertheless still deeply influenced in our apprehension of the world by the ideals and beliefs of the seventeenth century. As Alfred North Whitehead observed, some of the most fundamental ideas of what he termed 'the century of genius' are 'still reigning.'[8] Others have made similar observations.[9] For this reason, when we dissect Hobbes, we are likely to find that we are cutting upon some very live tissue. Understanding how he viewed the world can help us to recognize some of the matrices of our own perceptions. And since Hobbes is consciously aware of propositions which have since drifted into the level of tacit, hence unarticulated and unexamined, assumptions, reading him with understanding becomes an especially valuable experience in self-understanding.

Hobbes provides an especially fertile source of insight into our intellectual tradition, since the linkages to the Aristotelian components of the tradition can be recognized in him, even as he attacks the central substantive models of Aristotelianism. We therefore gain a further appreciation of the continuity of our intellectual tradition, and we can understand how Whitehead could say that 'science started its modern career by taking over ideas derived from the weakest side of the philosophies of Aristotle's successors.'[10]

Given the intrinsic fascination of Hobbes's ideas and the pivotal position which he occupies in the history of Western thought in general and Western political thought in particular, it is not surprising that a considerable variety of interpretations of his ideas have been expounded. The possibility of various interpretative emphases is also enhanced by some important problems and ambiguities in his corpus. Different pictures of Hobbes can emerge from different judgments as to what is central and what is peripheral in his work, and, in cases of apparent contradiction or superfluous multiple explanations, from different judgments as to what reflects his real intent. No single, final, and unequivocal account of the meaning and significance of Hobbes's political theory is therefore likely to arise. This is not necessarily a situation to be deplored, however. Profound and fecund thinkers will always contain heuristic possibilities which are not all mutually compatible simply because they touch profoundly the complexity of reality.

Hobbes's own contemporaries reacted to his thought with virtually unanimous horror. The clergy, Aristotelian and Platonic philosophers, divine right royalists, and lawyers all found Hobbes indigestible for a diversity of reasons. To one Norfolk divine, Hobbes was 'the hideous monstrosity and British beast, the Propagator of execrable doctrines, the Promulgator of mad wisdom, the Herald and Pugilist of impious death, the Insipid Venerator of a Material God, the Renowned Fabricator of a monocondyte Symbol, the Depraved Renewer of old heresies to the faith, the Nonsensical roguish vendor of falsifications.'[11] Like Machiavelli, Hobbes became a quasi-demonic symbol to most men of his time. His alleged atheism, his materialism, his political absolutism, his alleged libertinism all were perceived as bound up in one frightening package, potent but wholly unacceptable, worthy of being taken seriously but only as an adversary.

More recent commentary on Hobbes has tended to centre around two principal problems: the relationship of his political thought to other parts of his world view such as his natural philosophy, his psychology, and his rationalist methodology; and the structure of his theory of political obligation.

In his book on Hobbes published in 1886, George Croom Robertson took issue with the conventional assumption that Hobbes's political ideas had sprung from the womb of his philosophical materialism.[12] According to Robertson, Hobbes's historical and personal circumstances, rather than a more systematic and abstract philosophical doctrine, was the real source of his political ideas. 'More than of almost any other philosopher,' Robertson argued, 'it can be said of Hobbs that the key to a right understanding of his thought is to be found in his personal circumstances and the events of his time.'[13] Methodologically, said Robertson, Hobbes proceeded not by drawing out the implications of his general principles for politics, but rather by following up the consequences of what he directly had observed on a relatively *ad hoc* basis about human psychology and political realities. 'There can be little doubt, however Hobbes might wish by afterthought to connect his theory of political society with the principles of his general mechanical philosophy, that it sprang originally from a different line of consideration. Direct analysis of the notions of Justice and Law, in relation with such knowledge of human appetites and passions as any man "that will but examine his own mind" has by experience, remained for him always a sufficient basis for civil philosophy, without going deeper.'[14]

The problem to which Robertson directed his attention here is both interesting and vexing for several reasons. As a general problem, it is significant as one seeks to understand the structure of political theory which, in its classic form, often purports to make precisely the kind of connections between cosmology and sociology that Robertson minimizes in Hobbes. With specific relation to Hobbes himself, the problem is complicated by Hobbes's own apparent ambivalence on the issue. On one side of the question stands the fact that Hobbes wrote his *Philosophical Rudiments Concerning Government and Society* (*De Cive*) before writing *De Corpore* and *De Homine*, which treated the more fundamental principles of his general philosophy. If Hobbes's political ideas were in fact derived from his materialist philosophy, the logical, hence chronological, relationship should have been reversed.

Hobbes was aware of this problem. The departure from logical order, he said, was an outgrowth of the political situation; and it did not disturb him greatly because he felt that *De Cive* could stand by itself. 'Therefore it happens, that what was last in order, is yet come forth first in time. And the rather, because I saw that, grounded on its own principles sufficiently known by experience, it would not stand in need of the former sections.'[15] Since Hobbes himself attests that the principles of *De Cive* may be 'sufficiently known by experience,' then Robertson's view that Hobbes's attempt to ground his political ideas in his natural philosophy was an *ex post facto* gloss seems quite sustainable.

On the other hand, Hobbes clearly felt that a fundamental unity pervaded his work, that his political principles did have logical footing in his natural philosophy, and that the former depended upon the latter for their demonstrability. 'Such things as I have said are to be taught last (i.e., civil philosophy),' he wrote, 'cannot be demonstrated, till such as are propounded to be first treated of (i.e., natural philosophy) be fully understood.'[16] It is also clear, moreover, that even if *De Cive* preceded *De Corpore* and *De Homine*, Hobbes had previously articulated his basic principles of natural philosophy.[17] The order of publication of *De Cive*, *De Homine*, and *De Corpore* therefore cannot be taken as representative of the path by which Hobbes arrived at his conclusions. The problem remains a live one.

Agreeing with Robertson that 'the real basis of Hobbes's political philosophy is not modern science,' Leo Strauss argued that the actual foundation of Hobbes's political theory was his conception of natural right.[18] Strauss conceded that Hobbes explicitly wanted to ground his political theory on the new ideas of modern natural science, but, said Strauss, he was thereby engaged in intellectual self-delusion. Earlier theorists could draw political principles from cosmological models because their cosmologies contained human features such as purpose, meaning, and order. With the new cosmology, however, this connection could not be made because the cosmos of modern natural science was fundamentally ahuman. Hobbes therefore was engaging in the impossible task of trying to draw conclusions from utterly insufficient premises. In Strauss's words:

> As traditional moral and political philosophy was, to some extent, based on traditional metaphysics, it seemed necessary, when traditional metaphysics were replaced by modern natural science, to base the new moral and political philosophy on the new science. Attempts of this kind could never succeed: traditional metaphysics were, to use the language of Hobbes's successors, 'anthropomorphistic' and, therefore, a proper basis for a philosophy of things human; modern science, on the other hand, which tried to interpret nature by renouncing all 'anthropomorphisms,' all conceptions of purpose and perfection, could, therefore, to say the least, contribute nothing to the understanding of things human, to the foundation of morals and politics.[19]

Not only did Hobbes's preoccupation with natural philosophy not contribute to his political theory, Strauss continued, it actually was responsible for his confusions and apparent contradictions. By attempting the impossible Hobbes succeeded only in obscuring the true source of his principles of political obligation, namely the theory of natural right. Strauss went on to say that 'all the contradictions of any consequence' which occur in Hobbes may be explained as a product of the discrepancy between his 'original view of human life' and 'the conceptions provided by tradition or modern science.'[20] The task of the interpreter of Hobbes, therefore, is systematically to disentangle the scientific encumbrances from his ideas to reveal the fundamental coherence of his thought. The conception of natural right which provided the source of this coherence, Strauss argued, 'stands midway between strictly moral principles (such as those of the traditional natural law) on the one hand, and purely natural principles (such as pleasure, appetite, or even utility) on the other.'[21]

Strauss's elaboration of this basic thesis is both illuminating and provocative. At the same time, one must remain somewhat wary of an interpretative methodology which postulates a fundamental coherence to the ideas of a theorist and then proceeds to use that postulation as a standard to reject large chunks of the theorist's contentions as 'confused' or 'contradictory.' It is dangerous to separate on *a priori* grounds thoughts which their author clearly conceived to be interrelated. Shortly I shall argue that, while Strauss is illuminating in what he affirms about Hobbes, he is misleading in what he denies; and this difficulty stems from his overly narrow conception of the way in which one set of ideas can influence ideas about other realities.

A somewhat different approach to Hobbes's thought was taken by the distinguished British political theorist Michael Oakeshott, in his introduction to a new edition of *Leviathan* in 1947. Most interpretation of Hobbes, Oakeshott felt, was basically divided between two camps: those who saw Hobbes's thought as a single, materialistic system, and those who saw it as composed of two or more distinct and not wholly reconcilable components. Both of these views Oakeshott found inadequate. Hobbes's thought, Oakeshott argued, was indeed a coherent system; but, he argued, the nature and origin of the coherence and hence of the system itself had been fundamentally misconceived.

For Oakeshott, the unity of Hobbes's thought is not the unity of a logical pyramid, with each level systematically laid on top of the more basic propositions, but instead is the unity of a complex whole tied together by a cohering theme. And this unifying strand that runs throughout Hobbes's thought is a consistent conception of what philosophy is all about. 'The coherence of his philosophy, the system of it, lies not in an architectonic structure, but in a single passionate thought that pervades its parts. . . . And the thread, the hidden thought, is the continuous application of a doctrine about the nature of philosophy.'[22] In Oakeshott's view, Hobbes is systematic because he is consistently 'rationalist' in a particular sense: 'Philosophy for him is the world as it appears in the mirror of reason; civil philosophy is the image of the civil order reflected in that mirror.'[23] Oakeshott did not deny the mechanistic features of Hobbes's doctrine, but he argued that these were essentially derivative features which followed from Hobbes's conception of rational method. For Hobbes, the realm of reason is the realm of cause and effect. The operations of reason proper are to resolve and compose the object of analysis into its parts and to discover its antecedents and consequents. Anything not subject to this form of knowing is not the proper object of philosophy.[24] This, in effect, Oakeshott argued, is to make reasoning into the 'elucidation of mechanism' since it is essentially the study of the 'combination, transfer, and resolution of forces.'[25] The picture which Hobbes draws of politics is, therefore, part of an overall system, and this system is 'mechanical'; but the origin of both system and mechanism is the pervasive application of this particular conception of reason. Hobbes is systematic and mechanical, but these are traits derivative of a consistent and distinctive methodology, not autonomous substantive doctrines. 'The civil order is conceived as a coherence of powers, not because politics is vulgarly observed to be a competition of powers, or because civil philosophy must take its conceptions from natural philosophy, but because to subject the civil order to rational enquiry unavoidably turns it into a mechanism.'[26]

Oakeshott's interpretation has some genuine virtues. It brings out with clarity and force some of the peculiarities of Hobbes's conception of rational inquiry and demonstrates both that Hobbes took this conception quite seriously and that it therefore exercised a significant structuring impact upon his thought.

How he asked his questions, what he thought to be the requirements of 'rational' answers, left an undeniable mark on his
whole corpus. Moreover, this central observation by Oakeshott
is well worth generalizing beyond the particular case of Hobbes.
Too often methods are thought to be merely technical contri-
vances that may be devised, adopted, rejected, or exchanged
without having any significant impact on the form of the results.
Oakeshott's interpretation indicates that the impact of different
methods is not neutral, that in fact a particularly potent and
consistently applied methodology may deeply structure the
substance of the final theory. In political science, as well as in
other sciences, as students of 'scientific method' are now point-
ing out, an abstractive methodology possesses a real tendency
to generate its own ontology.[27]

Oakeshott nevertheless may well have overstated his case.
Hobbes's conception of reason played a significant part in shaping his doctrines, but it is questionable whether its impact was as
autonomous and dominant as Oakeshott indicated. In the first
place, there is always the question of how autonomous epistemology is in its relationship to ontology. Ever since Descartes,
there has been a strong tendency to focus upon epistemological
issues as central, but one can make a very good case that
epistemological and methodological revolutions actually rest
upon transformed visions of what is 'real'. That is, ontology is
logically prior to epistemology, since one who wishes to know
reality rather than to fabricate it must conform his approach to
that reality rather than vice versa.[28] Philosophical theorists and
scientific researchers alike may become fascinated with a particular method, but they do so out of a conviction, often warran-
ted by particularly striking cases, that the method is peculiarly
appropriate to the reality they wish to know. Otherwise, they
become like the drunk who looked for his wristwatch under the
lamppost where there was more light, even though he lost it in
the dark alley.

In the particular case of Hobbes, this line of argument has
added force if one examines carefully Oakeshott's account of

Hobbes's conception of reason and its consequences. Basically, Oakeshott argues that, first, 'reasoning,' for Hobbes, 'is concerned solely with causes and effects.'[29] Second, this doctrine means that reasoning, being a study of cause and effect, is essentially 'elucidation of mechanism.'[30] It therefore follows that a rational account of anything for Hobbes must have strong mechanistic overtones, however derivative they may be. The critical hidden assumption here, however, comes in the second premise: namely, it is assumed that an analysis of cause and effect is *ipso facto* a mechanistic analysis. This assumption is not itself logically necessary, nor is it methodologically derived; instead it depends upon a prior substantive assumption about the nature of causation. And, in fact, it was precisely a transformation in the understanding of causality that was one of the key elements in the transformed cosmology of the seventeenth century. Hobbes differs in his conception of rational inquiry from the Aristotelian tradition not in *that* he considers it intimately bound up with an account of cause and effect, but in *what* he saw to be genuinely causative. Therefore, Oakeshott's thesis as to the priority of rational method in the structure of Hobbes's thought is cast into question.

A somewhat distinctive strand of Hobbes's interpretation has been developed which insists upon the separation of Hobbes's psychological postulates and his political theory. A. E. Taylor provided the most important opening contribution to this approach to Hobbes in an article on 'The Ethical Doctrine of Hobbes,' published in 1938.[31] He contended there that 'Hobbes's ethical doctrine proper, disengaged from an egoistic psychology with which it has no logically necessary connection, is a very strict deontology, curiously suggestive, though with interesting differences, of some of the characteristic theses of Kant.'[32] In 1957 Howard Warrender published what must be considered the *magnum opus* of this interpretative standpoint, *The Political Philosophy of Hobbes: His Theory of Obligation*.[33] Warrender's argument differed from that of Taylor in some significant details, but it shared enough in common with

Taylor's view to generate the designation: the Taylor-Warrender thesis. The differences between Taylor and Warrender center mostly around the parallels which Taylor finds between Hobbes and Kant and also around the central significance which Taylor assigns to covenanting as a source of obligation.[34] The two agree on several fundamental contentions, however, which are both significant and controversial.

In the view of Taylor and Warrender, Hobbes's theory of political obligation must be separated analytically from his natural philosophy and his psychology. The principal grounds for this alleged analytical necessity are logical; that is, it is not logically possible to derive a moral theory from an empirical theory, an account of how men should behave from an account of how they do behave. If Hobbes thought he could do this, the contention runs, he was simply mistaken, and we must look elsewhere to see if a viable theory can be pieced together from his writings.

Specifically, Warrender argues, it would be impossible for Hobbes to assert the presence of a moral obligation to obey the will of the sovereign unless some basis of moral obligation exists prior to and beyond the institution of the sovereign. As he puts it, 'A moral obligation to obey the civil law cannot logically be extracted from a system in which man has no moral obligations before or apart from the institution of that law. Any view that assumes otherwise, contains a hiatus in the argument that cannot be surmounted, and if, in fact, this is Hobbes's position, he must be held to have failed in his main enterprise.'[35] It therefore follows that the presence of moral obligations must be found in the 'state of nature' (which represents the human condition antecedent to civil society) if Hobbes is to be granted as having any real theory of political obligation.

This requirement Hobbes is held to have satisfied with his account of the law of nature. He clearly distinguishes between law and counsel; only the former are fully obligatory in the strict sense. And Hobbes, as Taylor observes, 'always describes the items of the natural law as *dictamina*, or dictates, never as *consilia*, or pieces of advice.'[36] Therefore, the account often given of Hobbes's theory that makes political obligation derivative solely upon the *ipse dixit* of the sovereign is not accurate: 'Hobbes always lays it down that obligation is not created by the sovereign when he issues his orders backed by threats of penalties. The moral obligation to obey the natural law is antecedent to the existence of the legislator and the civil society.'[37] The law of nature is obligatory even in the state of nature, although it obliges only *in foro interno*. The existence of the sovereign, then, to use Warrender's term, is not the ground of political obligation, but merely one of the validating conditions. That is, the sovereign's will does not create obligation; his power merely renders an already existent obligation operative. Men are already obliged to 'seek peace and follow it' in the state of nature, but the insecurity of that state makes the obligation relatively ineffectual. By supplying security, and by serving as interpreter in disputed cases, the sovereign permits the obligation to take effect.

Alternative explanations are given by Taylor and Warrender as to why the laws of nature are obligatory. In one way or another, however, these explanations tend to emphasize the status of the laws of nature as commands of God. As Taylor says: 'I can only make Hobbes's statements consistent with one another by supposing that he meant quite seriously what he so often says, that the natural law is the command of God, and to be obeyed *because* it is God's command.'[38] This interpretation makes sense, given the premises, because Hobbes clearly equated law with command; hence, if natural laws are truly laws, they must be someone's commands, and if obligatory they must be the command of one who commands by right. God, clearly, as the omnipotent creator of nature, is the only logical candidate for this role.

The whole controversy surrounding the Taylor-Warrender thesis is extremely complex and tricky.[39] The difficulties here arise partly from ambiguities and complexities in Hobbes. They also arise from the ambiguities inherent in the notion of obligation itself. If one pauses to reflect upon the multitude of meanings that can be given the term oblige, he will understand this aspect of the problem. This whole issue warrants closer attention, but such attention falls beyond my scope here. The basic organizing hypothesis of this work does contain implications for this issue, however, and these will be unfolded in due course. For the moment, only the following caveat will be entered. Although the Taylor-Warrender thesis has illuminated some significant aspects of Hobbes's political theory, it has a clear tendency to change the overall image which Hobbes seemed to have of his own work. In the first place, it makes absolutely central what Hobbes deemed to be relatively peripheral — e.g. the status of laws of nature as divine commands — and makes peripheral what Hobbes deemed important — e.g. the relationship of self-interest and duty. Moreover, the whole thesis involves a laborious separation of what Hobbes equally laboriously strove to reconcile, namely, his psychological postulates and his account of the origin of political obligation. This transformation may be justified on the grounds that it is necessary to save Hobbes from the 'logical blemish'[40] of deriving an 'ought' from an 'is.' This justification, however, raises the question of how far one is entitled to interpret a person's thought after rejecting his premises. While this task may be a legitimate enterprise from the standpoint of abstract political theory, it makes questionable the historical accuracy of the conclusions reached. Finally, it is worth considering whether Hobbes's logical assumptions about the relationship of 'moral' and 'empirical' realities are as faulty as many modern thinkers so readily assume.

In contrast to the tendency of Strauss, Robertson, and Warrender to distinguish and disentangle allegedly logically unconnected parts of Hobbes's thought from each other, one recent commentator argues quite persuasively that these different strands do link up into a reasonably coherent system of ideas. In his 1965 study of Hobbes, J. W. N. Watkins concludes that the essentials of Hobbes's political theory are implied by his more general philosophical doctrines.[41] Watkins in effect contends that denials of the systematic features of Hobbes's thought stem from an overly rigid standard for accrediting ideas as systematic. A very real systematic connection of ideas can be present even though they do not form a simple system of axiomatic premises and logical deductions. As Watkins observes:

A philosophical proposition cannot by itself entail a proposition having a political content which the former lacks. But the introduction of a philosophical theory 'p' into an existing circle of statements 'q' may make it possible to derive a new political conclusion 'r'; in which case 'p' implies that if 'q' then 'r.' Moreover, if 'r' is controversial, whereas 'q' consists of uncontroversial background assumptions . . . then the philosophical idea bears the chief responsibility for the political conclusion, and the latter may be said, by a pardonable ellipsis, to be an *implication* of the philosophical idea.[42]

After examining the 'Tract on First Principles,' sometimes referred to as the 'Little Treatise,' which Hobbes wrote around 1630, Watkins concludes that 'Hobbes was a mechanical philosopher before the main lines of his political doctrine were fixed, and his early theorizing spilt over into his political theorizing.'[43] The basic ideas on cosmology, psychology, and ethics contained in the 'Little Treatise' persisted largely intact into Hobbes's later writings and play a significant role there.

In response to Warrender's painstaking attempt to sever a coherent theory of obligation from the larger pattern of Hobbes's philosophy, Watkins argues that 'Warrender mistook the theological top layer of a single system for a separate system existing alongside what is really its psychological or naturalistic basis.'[44] In deriving obligations from factual premises, Hobbes was not committing a simple logical *faux pas*, for the pattern of obligation he presents is not fundamentally a set of categorical imperatives. Instead, they are a framework of hypothetical imperatives, contingent on the presupposition that any man naturally will seek to preserve himself from a violent death. The prescriptive laws of nature which Hobbes offers his readers are not moral imperatives in the strict sense, but they are imperative nevertheless. In Watkins's words, 'they are more like doctor's orders of a peculiarly compelling kind.'[45] Their peculiarly compelling character, in turn, rests upon the givens of human nature and its constituent passions.

Sheldon Wolin finds himself largely in agreement both with Watkins and with Oakeshott. With the former, he agrees that 'scientific modes of thought had permeated (Hobbes's) political philosophy.'[46] Strauss's argument to the contrary, Wolin argues, is 'brilliant but overly ingenious.'[47] And, with Oakeshott, Wolin feels that central to Hobbes's enterprise is a pervasive and distinctive new type of methodological rationalism that shapes the form of his inquiry and influences his conclusions in the process.

Wolin places a distinctive and illuminating emphasis upon the role of stipulated rules in Hobbes's political thought. Hobbes, he observes, had to face up at the very outset of his work to the problem posed by the 'interest-ridden nature of the new politics,'[48] a problem brought into prominence by Machiavelli. The crucial and extreme manifestation of this breakdown in community was the dissolution of a commonly held political language. Since men interpreted meanings according to their own self-interest, the state of nature was 'a condition distraught by an anarchy of meanings.'[49] The most fundamental task of one who would lift men out of this chaotic condition, therefore, was to provide certain rules of correct belief and conduct which could deliver society from a morass of subjectivity—a subjectivity which found its behavioral expression in the 'war of all against all.'

The key to providing these certain rules Hobbes found in the methods of the new scientific philosophy, as he understood them. Hobbes's model for scientific method, as many commentators have noted, was heavily geometric. Thus, the methods of the new science were to provide the axioms needed for the political society and to make the necessary and proper deductions from them that would guide men's actions. 'Just as there were basic rules or conventions governing the usages of geometers, there were rules or propositions distinctive to political life and necessary for its survival.'[50]

Hobbes's philosophical nominalism prohibited him from appealing to some objective Reason as the source for the necessary rules. Therefore the problem of how these rules were to be stipulated converged with the explicitly political problem of authority; that is, political authority would inhere pre-eminently in epistemological authority. The source of co-herence in society must be a single voice which is empowered to lay down the basic political definitions of the society—the common framework of meanings to which each individual citizen must subscribe. This single voice was, of course, that of the sovereign, who based his sovereignty upon his fundamental role as a Great Definer. As Wolin puts it, 'the Hobbesian sovereign occupied a truly awesome position. He was the un-challengeable master of the system of rules or stipulative defini-tions fundamental to political peace.'[51]

Another interpretation argues that the central structuring element of Hobbes's political theory is sociological rather than philosophical. In his study of Hobbes, C. B. MacPherson offers a perceptive example of this approach as one variant of the political theory of 'possessive individualism.'[52] Like Rousseau, MacPherson contends that Hobbes's construct of the state of nature does not actually represent a genuinely presocial order, but instead retains traits which are products of social condition-ing.[53] Specifically, Hobbes's model of the state of nature, like all his models, is permeated by features of a competitive market society. It is the incorporation of this form of social order into his assumptions that provides one of the essential foundations of Hobbes's psychology, MacPherson contends: 'his postulate that the power of every man in society is opposed to the power of every other man requires the assumption of a model of society which permits and requires the continual invasion of every man by every other.'[54] Furthermore, the model of a competitive market society serves not only as the link between Hobbes's physiological postulates and his psychological doctrines but also as the basis of his theory of political obligation: 'The real basis of Hobbes's political obligation is . . . the rational perception of men in possessive market society that they are all irretrievably subject to the determination of the market.'[55] While this theory of obligation, built as it is upon a recognition and acceptance of the dynamics of a market, is not likely to be appealing to most humanist morality, MacPherson concludes, Hobbes nevertheless cut through to the heart of the politics of a competitive and individualistic bourgeois society.

This form of interpretation, centering as it does on the sociological determinants of Hobbes's theoretical model, probably tends to localize and constrict the significance of his thought more than is necessary. For example, contemporary ethological investigations into the sources of aggression in animal and human behavior would indicate that the *libido dominandi* is neither confined to, nor predominantly the product of, any particular form of social organization. Hobbes's model of human vainglory and quest for power, therefore, has more perennial relevance than MacPherson's analysis tends to imply. Nevertheless, it is also true that no social theorist writes in a sociopolitical vacuum, and some of Hobbes's ideas were in fact peculiarly applicable to the type of society which the commercial revolution was bringing to seventeenth-century England. MacPherson's analysis astutely points out this congruency and its significance both for our understanding of Hobbes and for our use of Hobbes to understand aspects of contemporary society.

This survey of various interpretations of Hobbes's thought is by no means exhaustive.[56] It does serve, however, to give an indication of some of the principal views which have been held.

Moreover, it also gives some indication of the principal issues which have generated controversy among Hobbes scholars. This tradition of Hobbes interpretation, finally, provides a suitable background against which the distinctive features of the account presented in the following chapters can be discerned.

The ideas of writers like Hobbes are too multifaceted to be encompassed in any single interpretation. Moreover, the ideas of a truly profound writer generally possess meanings and implications which even they themselves could not have seen or articulated. In theoretical inquiry, especially, it is true, as Michael Polanyi has said, that 'we say more than we know.' These heuristic features of important theoretical frameworks are, of course, not defects, but rather an index of their value. They do, however, make interpretative efforts more difficult and make humility an appropriate stance for the interpreter.

Although the interpretations cited offer a range of genuine insights into Hobbes, there remain some important characteristics of his philosophy which have not been given systematic exposition. These characteristics, furthermore, are not peripheral aspects of his thought which heretofore have been overlooked because of their relative triviality, but are some central constitutive and structuring elements of his fundamental world view. Understanding these aspects of Hobbes's philosophy provides not only a better understanding of the substance of his thought but also insight into some of the central conceptual models of Western intellectual history and greater appreciation of the formal process of political theorizing in the classical mode.

This study focuses largely upon the relationship of natural philosophy and political philosophy in Hobbes. My view, like that of Watkins, is that there is considerable interaction between the two and that the results of this interaction are significant for the final content of Hobbes's political theory. The impact of Hobbes's natural philosophy upon his political philosophy is not the product of purely deductive derivation.

As Leo Strauss correctly observed in his study of Hobbes, this kind of relationship is simply a logical impossibility. If there is no human substance in a natural cosmology, there is no way to deduce the content of a political cosmos from it. The human mind works in many ways other than deduction, however; and it is consequently quite conceivable that theories which cannot be related deductively may be related significantly in other ways. I hope that some of these other ways will be illuminated in the following chapters.

The focus of any study in political theory tends to be in large part a function of the author's view of what is the central task of political theory. This particular case is no exception to the general pattern. The implicit view of political theory which has helped to structure the focus of this particular inquiry is that, classically and properly, the central task of political theory is to relate sociology and cosmology, or at least to relate politics and human nature. In other words, the political theorist is one who examines the implications for political order of a pattern of order which contains but transcends the realm of politics. It is clear that political order is not purely autonomous and insulated from other patterns of order — whether the ecological order of the environment, the moral order of divine will, or the emotional order of the human psyche. Distinctive views of these transpolitical patterns of order will inevitably have a structuring impact upon views of politics. The case of Hobbes should be taken as an example of, not an exception to, this general contention.

Certainly it cannot be contested that Hobbes was nurtured, however reluctantly, by a tradition of political speculation which insisted upon making such connections between political order and cosmological order. This tradition therefore must be taken into account when trying to understand Hobbes. The human intelligence, Descartes notwithstanding, is incapable of beginning inquiry utterly devoid of presuppositions. As a result, even the most revolutionary thinker will retain certain assumptions of the tradition against which he is reacting. These assumptions are largely tacit, serving not as the focus of inquiry but rather as the footing or the conceptual grounding of inquiry. The thinker himself may not even be particularly aware of the assumptions, either because he takes them so largely for granted or simply because the specific object of his intellectual concern lies elsewhere. They are, nevertheless, important in shaping his final intellectual product in spite of their relative neglect as focal points of inquiry; indeed, they may be even more pervasive in their impact precisely because of their tacit status.

The intellectual tradition in which Hobbes was instructed and against which he reacted was thoroughly infused with Aristotelian premises. As a student at Oxford from 1603 to 1608, Hobbes's principal course of study was Aristotelian logic and Aristotelian physics. Like many other seventeenth-century figures who soon were to become exponents of the intellectual revolution of that century, Hobbes found the problems and concepts of Aristotelian scholasticism generally barren and uninteresting. After leaving Oxford, therefore, he largely abandoned philosophy for humanistic and historical studies. He did not re-enter the philosophical arena until Galileo had opened for him 'the gate to natural philosophy'; and when he did so, Aristotle was clearly an explicit object of attack. Along with his compatriots in the 'scientific revolution,' Hobbes happily jettisoned Aristotle as unproductive and obscurantist. 'I believe,' he wrote in the *Leviathan*, 'that scarce anything can be more absurdly said in natural Philosophy, than that which is called Aristotle's *Metaphysiques*, nor more repugnant to Government, than much of what he hath said in his *Politiques*; nor more ignorantly than a great part of his *Ethiques*.'[57]

Despite this vehement outburst, Hobbes clearly considered Aristotle an important philosophical antagonist. He does not merely dismiss him out of hand, but is constantly engaged in shaping his own contentions by contrasting them with corresponding Aristotelian notions. If Hobbes is explicitly in revolt against Aristotle, then, his work is nevertheless heavily shaped by, indeed saturated by, the very Aristotelian framework whose content he is rejecting. Almost all commentators on Hobbes have noted the presence of Aristotle in Hobbes's mind at one point or another in his writings. Together, these observations comprise an impressive list.

To begin with, Leo Strauss has demonstrated how closely Hobbes structured his anthropological reflections upon corresponding reflections in Aristotle's *Rhetoric*. In passage after passage, Hobbes replicates the form and sometimes the content of Aristotle's observations about the human passions. Strauss concludes: 'It would be difficult to find another classical work whose importance for Hobbes's political philosophy can be compared with that of the *Rhetoric*. The central chapters of Hobbes's anthropology, those chapters on which, more than on anything else he wrote, his fame as a stylist and as one who knows men rests for all time, betray in style and contents that the author was a zealous reader, not to say a disciple of the *Rhetoric*.'[58]

In regard to his natural philosophy Hobbes's ideas were governed closely by Aristotelian speculations, even where they were rejected.[59] In considering the problem of sensation, which Hobbes clearly conceived to be centrally important, Hobbes draws upon Aristotle in several ways. He assumes, for example, that touching is a necessary condition for things to influence each other, an assumption which, as Brandt observes, 'is an old Aristotelian conception.'[60] The supplementary conceptions of agent and patient which Hobbes 'would certainly have considered as being self-evident' are 'of Aristotelian origin.'[61] Hobbes also follows in the Aristotelian tradition with his formal definitions and the alleged implications of substance and accident. He, in Brandt's words, 'takes the Aristotelian conceptions, accident and substance, and consistently maintains them.'[62]

When Hobbes turns to the problem of the relationship of time, instant, and local motion, once again his speculations depend upon Aristotle's ideas. Brandt states: 'Hobbes's text is not understood from the context. Comprehension must be sought historically, and the explanation lies in Aristotelian premises.'[63] Considering the relationship of motion to that which attracts it, Hobbes relies upon Aristotle's definition of good as that toward which all things are moved. Hobbes makes some important changes in the Aristotelian notion of the good, as later will become evident, but the basic formal definition is clearly modeled upon Aristotle.[64] Brandt concludes his treatment of the 'Little Treatise,' in light of these considerations, by arguing that Aristotle predominates among the sources of Hobbes's basic conceptions. Aristotle, 'to a degree which is now difficult to realize, dominated the philosophy of that age.' He was 'the solid foundation, which one either tried to add to . . . or tried to pull down.'[65] In his philosophy of nature, Brandt demonstrates, just as Strauss showed with respect to his philosophical anthropology, Hobbes was no exception to this pattern.

Similarly, Richard Peters points out that Aristotelian concepts strongly influenced Hobbes's ideas about human thought processes. When Hobbes turned to consider 'trains of thought,' Peters observes, he, 'for all his devotion to the new sciences, was more influenced in his account by Aristotle than by mechanics.'[66] Moreover, 'Hobbes's account of regulated thinking owed a lot to and was an improvement on Aristotle's analysis of deliberation.'[67] Quite recently, Morton Kaplan wrote that 'despite his supposed modernity, Hobbes accepted Aristotle's definition of the theoretical but differed with him primarily in claiming that politics was a theoretical subject.'[68]

In light of all these indications of the impact of Aristotelian ideas upon Hobbes's thought, it is not surprising to find Howard Warrender writing in the preface to his *The Political Philosophy of Hobbes*: 'I had hoped originally to provide some historical explanation of Hobbes's views, and such material as I had collected to this end suggested that Hobbes's dependence upon Aristotle is even greater than has been supposed, despite Hobbes's own protests against his Aristotelian studies in

Oxford.'[69] Warrender, however, excluded this material from his study on the grounds that he was interested not so much 'with the problem of how Hobbes's theory originated or how it is to be explained, than with the prior question of what his theory is.'[70] Although quite in accord with Warrender's belief that understanding what Hobbes's theory *is* is more important than tracing its intellectual genealogy, I believe this distinction presents too simple a dichotomy. Only by understanding both *that* Aristotelian concepts are important in Hobbes and *how* they are important, do we really understand what his theory *is*. In other words, the question of Hobbes's relationship to Aristotelian ideas is one of intellectual substance, not simply one of intellectual pedigree.

It is not really sufficient for an adequate understanding of Hobbes and his indebtedness to Aristotle to compile a list of the ways in which the two philosophers are in agreement and a corresponding list of their differences. In some ways, such a compilation is illuminating, but only rather peripherally. It is requisite, instead, to perceive whether there is any systematic pattern to the relationship. If there is such a systematic pattern, then understanding it becomes fairly central to appreciating the vision of the thinker who was responsible for creating and using the pattern; if not, then the relationship becomes considerably more fortuitous and less interesting. The thesis of this study is that Hobbes's world view does exhibit quite a systematic relationship to the Aristotelian model of the world and that the logic and coherence of Hobbes's thought is therefore brought into relief by perceiving the structure of this relationship.

Hobbes was quite consciously and systematically engaged in a task of radically transforming a traditional cosmological paradigm. This paradigm transformation, when completed, moreover, inevitably carried with it some significant implications for political theorizing, partly because the corresponding implications of the original paradigm had been consciously drawn out by some of its adherents.

The notion of paradigm transformation calls for some

elaboration. The term paradigm is borrowed and adapted somewhat from the meaning given it by Thomas Kuhn in his *The Structure of Scientific Revolutions*.[71] Other terms could conceivably serve the same purpose, but this one has the advantage of a previous systematic elaboration and the derivative advantage of being a somewhat familiar concept. As Kuhn points out, every mature science proceeds on the basis of certain fundamental models of order which provide the systematic grounding for the basic concepts and methods of the discipline. Without such a model, or paradigm, the threshold of coherence and organization necessary to sustain organized inquiry and discourse would be lacking. From time to time, the fundamental paradigm, or paradigms, of a discipline become an insufficient framework for the fruitful investigation and interpretation of the problems faced by the discipline. The discipline then faces a kind of theoretical crisis which cannot be resolved until a new model or paradigm is devised which can both perform the functions of the old one and at the same time satisfactorily accommodate the perceptions which were anomalous for its predecessor. Scientific revolutions, Kuhn concludes, are best understood as instances of this kind of supplantation of one fundamental paradigm by another.

This concept of a fundamental paradigm and its functions is quite applicable beyond the scope of science, narrowly defined. It is both meaningful and illuminating to speak of a cosmological paradigm, for example: that is, a basic model of the fundamental realities of the cosmos and their interrelationship. In fact, the speculations of the great Greek cosmologists were precisely of this sort; they wished to supply a basic pattern or framework which could make intelligible the basic pattern of order in nature as a whole. In the early seventeenth-century tradition which served as the background of the scientific revolution, the cosmological paradigm had been supplied by Aristotle. His speculations provided the basic matrix for intellectual inquiry into the structure of the universe, a characterization of the basic realities of the world, and a format of how they were related to each other. This Aristotelian cosmological paradigm possessed the virtues of breadth of scope, depth, and coherence; and these features combined to give the model a profound and pervasive potency.

This Aristotelian cosmological model is what Hobbes sets out systematically to transform. The structure of this transformation bears some elaboration in the abstract before its concrete documentation, especially since the nature of the change is somewhat more complex than the pattern of revolution described by Kuhn. In the typical situation which Kuhn analyzes, one paradigm is substituted for another. The classic illustration of this phenomenon is the abandonment of the Ptolemaic model of astronomical movements for the Copernican model. In some cases, the previously accepted paradigm may be retained in a limited capacity; for example, the Newtonian model continues to have its genuine use, but only when applied to a limited situation within the more comprehensive Einsteinian model. These classic cases could be called, respectively, examples of paradigm *replacement* and paradigm *transcendence*. The movement from Aristotle's cosmos to the world of Thomas Hobbes shares common features with these examples, but it has features peculiar to it which warrant the designation of paradigm *transformation*.

The broad-ranging cosmological paradigm of Aristotelian discourse was not a single, simple model. It is more fruitful to conceive of it as composed of at least two levels related to each other by a kind of functional complementarity. The distinction between these two levels and the nature of their relationship is perhaps best characterized in terms which Michael Polanyi has employed in his epistemological reflections.[72] He argues that an analytically significant distinction can be made between 'tacit' and 'explicit' or between 'focal' and 'subsidiary' components in the operations of the human intelligence. These functionally related components are features both of visual perception and theoretical conception. In both of these cognitive operations, the human mind relies upon beliefs, assumptions, underlying patterns of order, as a footing from which to attend to its conscious concerns. In a particular cognitive act, the footing is functionally 'subsidiary' and the concerns are functionally 'focal.' Because the mind relies upon, rather than concentrates upon, the underlying framework of assumptions, these may also be characterized as 'tacit' components of knowledge in contrast with the 'explicit' components which are the object of attention. The designations of tacit and explicit are not attributes permanently affixed to any particular ideas, but are designations of functional roles which may be shifted according to the demands of the situation.

Numerous examples of this pattern are easy to cite from various manifestations of the human intellect. Both conceptually and perceptually, for example, it could be said that we rely upon certain tacit assumptions about space and time which serve to orient us in our observations of day-to-day events. Kant's categories of the understanding perform in this manner. Linguistically, we rely upon particular words or sounds in order to attend to the complex thought which they are being used to convey. If the mind instead turns to focus upon what should be the subsidiary features of the complex whole, then the thought is dissolved, as when, late at night, one is apt to complain that his tired eyes are reading 'just words.' Complex bodily achievements, which also are intelligent acts, exhibit the same pattern, as when a tennis player relies upon his grip, stance, and stroke in order to attend to the flight of the ball. As any tennis player can attest, this skilled operation also dissolves if the appropriate tacit-explicit relationship is abrogated. From his analysis, Polanyi concludes that the tacit dimension performs an irreducible role in all aspects of human knowledge.

The significance of Polanyi's analysis in the present context is that the Aristotelian cosmological paradigm was a complex whole whose various components, when deployed, were often functionally related in the focal-subsidiary pattern described. For our present purposes, I shall distinguish as one component of the Aristotelian paradigm what may be designated the tacit matrix. This component includes a number of assumptions about what the principal constituent features of the universe are and what their relationship is to each other. It is a matrix because it is a kind of structuring framework within which somewhat more localized problems about the nature of reality may be pursued. It is designated tacit in this context not because of its essential properties (for tacit and explicit are functional rather than essential designations), but because of the role that it plays in Hobbes's thought. The other component may be designated the focal model. This component is the basic analogy used, within the framework of the tacit matrix, to characterize reality. It answers the question 'what is reality like?' more than the question 'what is the underlying framework of things?' It is here characterized as focal because it was the conscious object of Hobbes's attention.

The relationship of Hobbes's cosmological paradigm to the Aristotelian paradigm can now be stated in the following way: Hobbes accepted the underlying framework of the Aristotelian paradigm, and this component was perpetuated in his thought as the tacit matrix of his own paradigm. He rejected, however, the focal model of the Aristotelian paradigm and replaced it with quite a different model which he found more satisfactory. This overall pattern may be characterized, then, as a paradigm transformation — a change in which the paradigm is systematically altered, but altered within the channels established by the original paradigm. In such a transformation, the resultant paradigm is a hybrid of the old and the new; the influence of the older paradigm persists, even though its face has been changed beyond recognition.[73]

This pattern of interpretation goes a long way, I believe, toward resolving some of the apparent paradoxes of Hobbes's thought and its relationship to the Aristotelian tradition. On the one hand, many analysts have noted the persistence of Aristotelian concepts and approaches throughout Hobbes's writings. At the same time, it is clear from Hobbes's explicit statements and from even a cursory reading of his work that there is a radical departure from the Aristotelian tradition in progress. Distinguishing between the different functional levels of the Aristotelian paradigm reconciles this apparent contradiction by explaining how it is possible for Hobbes to be both heavily Aristotelian in some ways and adamantly anti-Aristotelian in other respects. The pro- and anti-Aristotelian features are not simply conflicting items to be serially recounted, but instead comprise the systematically related particulars of two distinct functional levels of a single, complex intellectual model.

The constituents of both the focal and the tacit components of Hobbes's revolutionary cosmological paradigm will be unfolded in the chapters which follow. To a certain extent, the persistence of the Aristotelian framework as the tacit matrix of Hobbes's system of ideas will be exemplified as much as it will be stated. That is, it is reflected throughout in the systematic parallelism which holds between the exposition of Hobbes's ideas and the exposition of the corresponding Aristotelian notions against which he was reacting. It is possible, however, to state more explicitly, if rather sketchily, some of the assumptions which continue to form this persistent tacit framework. Hobbes, just as much as Aristotle, would have given his assent to a series of propositions which runs roughly as follows:

1. The created order of the world may be designated by the term nature.
2. Nature is a unified whole, with the same fundamental principles operative throughout.
3. Man himself is a part of nature; in fact, he is 'that Rationall and most excellent worke of Nature.'[74]
4. The constituents of nature are a) change, or motion, b) substance, or that which remains constant through change, c) accidents, or the perishable attributes of substance (although Hobbes considers figure and extension to be peculiar accidents in that they cannot perish without the body in which they inhere perishing also).[75]

5. Methodologically, one must understand nature by looking at its simplest elements, primary conditions, and first principles.
6. Among these first principles, the nature of motion is of peculiar importance, for it must be understood before nature can be understood.

These propositions indicate the basic structure of the tacit framework of the Aristotelian paradigm which persists into Hobbes's ideas. The revolutionary component of Hobbes's system grows from the radically different focal model which he develops in answer to the questions 'what is the pattern of motion; and what does remain through change?' Derivatively, he is led to give a correspondingly radical answer to the question 'is nature ordered and, if so, how?' And, finally, a very different kind of answer from that given by Aristotle is given to the problem 'what must man do to accommodate his political life to the realities of natural forces?' The answers to these questions form the central parts of Hobbes's world view. Moreover, they are interrelated answers, with the most basic answers exercising a profound influence on the answers provided the larger and more complex questions. This pattern of systematic relationship is mirrored in the organization of the following chapters, which, reflecting the tacit similarities between Aristotle and Hobbes, has a form appropriate to the exposition of the ideas of either and which elaborates the explicit differences that occur within this common framework. The analysis begins, then, where Hobbes, as Aristotle before him, began his analysis, namely, with an inquiry into the nature of motion.

NOTES

1. 'Introduction,' to the *Leviathan* (Oxford: Basil Blackwell, 1947), p. viii.
2. *The Political Philosophy of Hobbes*, trans. Elsa M. Sinclair (Chicago: University of Chicago Press, 1952), p. 1.

3. From the 'Foreword' to *Hobbes Studies*, ed. Keith C. Brown (Cambridge, Mass.: Harvard University Press, 1965), p. vii.

4. Howard Warrender, *The Political Philosophy of Hobbes* (Oxford: Clarendon Press, 1957); Keith C. Brown, ed., *Hobbes Studies*; Samuel Mintz, *The Hunting of Leviathan* (Cambridge, Eng.: Cambridge University Press, 1962); F. C. Hood, *The Divine Politics of Thomas Hobbes* (Oxford: Clarendon Press, 1964); J. W. N. Watkins, *Hobbes's System of Ideas* (London: Hutchinson University Library, 1965); M. M. Goldsmith, *Hobbes's Science of Politics* (New York: Columbia University Press, 1966); F. S. McNeilly, *The Anatomy of Leviathan* (New York: St. Martins Press, 1968); David P. Gauthier, *The Logic of Leviathan* (Oxford: Clarendon Press, 1969). One might also include in this list C. B. Macpherson's *The Political Theory of Possessive Individualism* (Oxford: Clarendon Press, 1962).

5. See Robert Dahl, *Modern Political Analysis* (Englewood Cliffs, N.J.: Prentice-Hall, 1963), p. 113.

6. See Richard Peters, *Hobbes* (London: Penguin Books, 1956), esp. pp. 135–37.

7. *The New Leviathan* (Oxford: Clarendon Press, 1942), p. iv.

8. *Science and the Modern World* (New York: Mentor Books, 1948), p. 55.

9. See for example Gerald J. Holton, ed., *Science and the Modern Mind* (Boston: Beacon Press, 1958).

10. *Science and the Modern World*, p. 23.

11. Quoted by Samuel I. Mintz, *The Hunting of Leviathan* (Cambridge: Cambridge University Press, 1962), p. 56. This excellent little survey and John Bowles's *Hobbes and His Critics* (London: Jonathan Cape, 1951) are the best introductions to the reactions of Hobbes's contemporaries to his ideas.

12. *Hobbes* (Edinburgh: William Blackwood and Sons, 1886).

13. Ibid., pp. v-vi.

14. Ibid., p. 138.

15. Thomas Hobbes, *English Works*, ed. William Molesworth

(London: John Bohn, 1839), Vol. II, xx; hereafter cited as *English Works*.

16. Hobbes, *English Works*, 1: 87–88.

17. Especially in 'The Little Treatise,' uncovered by Ferdinand Tönnies. See Frithiof Brandt, *Thomas Hobbes's Mechanical Conception of Nature* (Copenhagen: Levin and Munksgaard, 1928), chapt. 1.

18. *The Political Philosophy of Hobbes* (Chicago: University of Chicago Press, 1952), p. ix. (Page references are to the Phoenix edition.)

19. Ibid., p. ix.

20. Ibid., p. xi.

21. Ibid., p. viii.

22. (Oxford: Basil Blackwell, 1947), p. xix.

23. Ibid., p. xx.

24. See Hobbes, *English Works*, 1:10.

25. Oakeshott, 'Introduction,' p. xxi.

26. Ibid., p. xxi.

27. See Marx W. Wartofsky, *The Conceptual Foundations of Modern Science* (New York: Macmillan Co., 1969), p. 361.

28. See Karl Mannheim, *Essays on the Sociology of Knowledge*, ed. Paul Kecskemeti (New York: Oxford University Press, 1952): 'Although epistemology claims to furnish a standard in terms of which the truth of metaphysical systems can be judged, it turns out itself to have its basis in definite metaphysical positions' (p. 112).

29. *Oakeshott*, 'Introduction,' p. xx.

30. Ibid., p. xxi.

31. *Philosophy* 13 (1938): 406–24.

32. Ibid., p. 408.

33. (Oxford: Clarendon Press, 1957).

34. See the Appendix to Warrender, *The Political Philosophy of Hobbes*.

35. Warrender, *The Political Philosophy of Hobbes*, p. 6.

36. Taylor, 'The Ethical Doctrine of Hobbes,' p. 411.

37. Ibid., p. 412.

38. Ibid., p. 417.

39. See for example the sample arguments included in Brown, ed., *Hobbes Studies*.

40. Richard Peters, *Hobbes*, p. 161.

41. *Hobbes's System of Ideas* (London: Hutchinson University Library, 1965). M. M. Goldsmith reaches a generally similar conclusion in *Hobbes's Science of Politics* (New York: Columbia University Press, 1966).

42. Watkins, *Hobbes's System of Politics*, p. 24.

43. Ibid., p. 29.

44. Ibid., p. 95.

45. Ibid., p. 76.

46. Sheldon S. Wolin, *Politics and Vision* (Boston: Little, Brown and Co., 1960), pp. 281–82.

47. Ibid., p. 478. 'What is troublesome about [Strauss's] interpretation,' he continues, 'is not only that there were precious few political comments in [Hobbes's early "humanist" writings] to justify the elaborate edifice constructed by Strauss, but that [his argument] also involves a cavalier dismissal of *A Short Tract on First Principles* which belonged to the same "humanist" period' (pp. 478–79).

48. Ibid., p. 240.

49. Ibid., p. 257.

50. Ibid., p. 254.

51. Ibid., p. 266.

52. *The Political Theory of Possessive Individualism* (Oxford: Clarendon Press, 1962).

53. Rouseau wrote in his *Discourse on the Origin of Inequality* that Hobbes was one of those 'who, in reasoning on the state of nature, always import into it ideas gathered in a state of society' (Everyman's Library [New York: E. P. Dutton Co., 1950], p. 214). Specifically, the egoism and vanity which Hobbes depicts as a characteristic of natural man, Rousseau sees as a 'purely relative' feeling which could arise only in society. 'In the true state of nature,' he concludes, 'egoism did not exist' (Ibid., p. 223).

54. *The Political Theory of Possessive Individualism*, p. 42.

55. Ibid., p. 106.

56. The interested reader can find some further distinctive insights as well as occasional controversial suggestions, in the following works: Raymond Polin, *Politique et Philosophie chez Thomas Hobbes* (Paris: Presses Universitaires de France, 1953); F. S. McNeilly, *The Anatomy of Leviathan*; M. M. Goldsmith, *Hobbes's Science of Politics*; David P. Gauthier, *The Logic of Leviathan*; and F. C. Hood, *The Divine Politics of Thomas Hobbes*.

Polin's work is a general study which contains a helpful analysis of Hobbes's theory of representation. McNeilly offers an illuminating discussion of the pattern of change and development in Hobbes's thought from his earlier to his final work. Goldsmith emphasizes the continuity among the different components of Hobbes's thought. Gauthier turns the tools of logical analysis upon Hobbes's moral and political doctrines. And Hood presents an arguable picture of Hobbes as largely a traditional Christian moralist, inspired principally by scripture, even though he was Euclidean in his method and materialist in his ontology.

57. P. 589.

58. *The Political Philosophy of Hobbes*, p. 35.

59. Brandt, *Thomas Hobbes's Mechanical Conception of Nature*.

60. Ibid., p. 13.

61. Ibid.

62. Ibid., p. 17.

63. Ibid., p. 26. The largely tacit role of Aristotle's conceptions appears clearly in Brandt's analysis. 'It is characteristic that the interlinks of this reasoning, viz. Aristotle's conception of time and instant and motion, is not mentioned at all. It has evidently appeared to Hobbes as unnecessary. At the bottom of his exposition lies something in this direction: If species move in an instant then they do not move locally—for who is ignorant of the fact that Aristotle has irrefutably demonstrated that in an instant no movement can take place' (p. 27).

64. See ibid., p. 45.

65. Ibid., p. 55.

66. *Hobbes*, p. 113.

67. Ibid., p. 115.

68. Morton A. Kaplan, *Macropolitics* (Chicago: Aldine Publishing Co., 1969), pp. 5–6.

69. P. viii.

70. Ibid., pp. viii-ix.

71. (Chicago: Phoenix Books, 1961).

72. See *Personal Knowledge* (London: Routledge and Kegan Paul, 1958) and *The Tacit Dimension* (Garden City, N.Y.: Doubleday, 1966).

73. Recently, Kuhn and some of his more astute interpreters have taken similar steps to break down the notion of the 'paradigm' into its distinguishable constituent elements. See Kuhn's 'Postscript' to the second edition of *Structure of Scientific Revolutions* (Chicago: Univ. of Chicago Press, 1970) and Margaret Masterman, 'The Nature of a Paradigm' in *Criticism and the Growth of Knowledge*, ed. Imre Lakatos and Alan Musgrave (Cambridge, Eng., Cambridge University Press, 1970). See also the discussion in the Conclusion to this study.

74. *Leviathan*, p. 3.

75. See *English Works*, 1:104.

2

Inertia and the End of the Finite Cosmos

'The fulfillment of what exists potentially, in so far as
it exists potentially, is motion.' — *Aristotle*

'Motion is nothing but change of place.' — *Hobbes*

Vast conceptual revolutions often turn around very small
hinges. The intellectual revolution of the seventeenth century,
which shattered the medieval synthesis of Christianity and
Aristotelianism, can be taken as a striking instance of this sort.
It would, of course, be a gross oversimplification to attribute
such a remarkable intellectual cataclysm to the transformation
of a single concept. Nevertheless, the more that one examines
the logical structure of the seventeenth-century intellectual
transformation, the more he is impressed by the absolute
centrality to the whole process of a new view of motion. As
Herbert Butterfield has observed: 'Of all the intellectual
hurdles which the human mind has confronted and has overcome in the last fifteen hundred years, the one which seems to
me to have been the most amazing in its character and the most
stupendous in the scope of its consequences is the one relating
to the problem of motion.'[1]

This radical and important change in the understanding of
how things move was a genuine paradigm switch of the kind
described by Kuhn. It was a change in the way that people
looked at things that went right to the fundamentals of conceptualization — so deep that it constituted a perceptual
'gestalt shift' such as those described by psychologists of
perception.[2] What those who had become conceptually
reoriented looked at — the data — were the same phenomena as

before, but what they actually saw was something quite different. The change was in many ways as sudden as it was profound, for a gestalt shift is not accomplished simply by the addition of a new piece of data, but instead happens all at once, just as the eye instantaneously may transform the famous 'duck-rabbit' sketch now into a duck and then back into a rabbit (see figure 1).

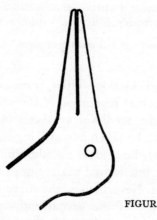

FIGURE I

Butterfield analogizes this process of profound intellectual reorientation to picking up the opposite end of the stick, and he points out how pervasive the implications of such a change can be. In the case of the transformed view of motion,

> it altered much of one's ordinary thinking about the world and opened the way for a flood of further discoveries and reinterpretations, even in the realm of common sense, before any very elaborate experiments had been embarked upon. It was as though science or human thought had been held up by a barrier until this moment—the waters dammed because of an initial defect in one's attitude to everything in the universe that had any sort of motion—and now the floods were released. Change and discovery were bound to come in cascades even if there were no other factors working for a scientific revolution.[3]

Hobbes's infatuation with the whole problem of motion exudes from practically all his philosophical and political works. He was, as Richard Peters has said, 'a man almost bemused by the wonder of motion.'[4] The *Leviathan* is ostensibly a treatise on politics, but Hobbes thinks it logical and appropriate to begin with a consideration of sensation, in which he alleges sensible qualities to be 'but so many several motions of the matter.'[5] He is only a couple of pages into his subject, moreover, before he is immersed in a discussion of the principle of inertia. All this intrusion of the problem of motion into places the modern reader would deem to be unlikely can be rather puzzling, but it reflects the accuracy of the characterization of Hobbes as 'the great metaphysician of motion.'[6] Any account of Hobbes's thought, therefore, must begin by examining the substance of, and the reasons behind, this infatuation with motion. Only after such an examination can the implications of Hobbes's natural philosophy for his political theory be assessed knowledgeably.

The problem of change, or motion, was not novel in the seventeenth century. In fact, the cosmological speculations of the Greeks which provided the starting point for both the philosophical and the scientific traditions in the West centered very largely around this problem. Parmenides and Heraclitus had posed the problem of the reality of change by taking essentially polar positions on the question. For the one, nothing ever really changed, while for the other change was the only reality. The task of resolving this antinomy was taken up by Plato, and it led him into the formulation of some of his most profound and characteristic cosmological ideas. The famous Platonic theory of the Forms, in fact, was the foundation of the answer he provided to the riddle of change and permanence. The Forms themselves were unchangeable, immutable, eternal. They supplied the vehicle of cosmic stability and permanence within which change, which was also real, took place. The Ideas were the 'really real' constituents of the cosmos, but the flux of phenomenal existence had reality as well, by virtue of participation in these Ideas.

The Aristotelian model of motion which persisted with such profound influence into the medieval scholasticism of Western Europe owed a great deal to this Platonic formulation. True, Aristotle attacked the Platonic doctrine of Forms, but this assault was not against the concept of Forms itself, but against what Aristotle felt was Plato's tendency to view the Forms as existing in some eternal realm wholly outside the phenomenal world. His concern was not to repudiate the Forms, but, quite the contrary, to explain how they are effectual; for if the Forms were transcendent, Aristotle argued, they would be irrelevant. As he says in the *Metaphysics*: 'Again, it would seem impossible that the substance and that of which it is the substance should exist apart; how, therefore, could the Ideas, being the substances of things, exist apart?'[7] Having rejected the transcendence of the Forms as an impossibility, Aristotle brought the Forms within the sensible world of things. The naturalized, immanent Forms are the 'substances' which give order and coherence to the world. 'For the substance is the indwelling form,' says Aristotle, 'from which and the matter the so-called concrete substance is derived.'[8]

This theory of immanent forms provides the setting for the Aristotelian model of motion, for substance is that which remains unmoved within a process of change. 'In respect of substance there is no motion.'[9] Movement, then, is visualized as something which takes place within the immutable boundaries of immanent form. Therefore, movement is limited and finite. Change has a definite beginning and an equally definite end, with this end in fact constituting an irreducible cause of the motion. 'Every change,' as Aristotle says, 'is *from* something *to* something, as the word itself [*metabole*] indicates.'[10] This formulation then leads Aristotle to his famous definition of motion as the synapse of potential to actual. In the *Physics*, Aristotle gives this definition in the following way: 'The fulfillment of what exists potentially, in so far as it exists potentially, is *motion*.'[11] This model of motion is well known, but its extensive and important implications are often not fully appreciated. These implications warrant some exploration, for they go a long way toward filling in the structure of the cosmological model which governed Western thought into the seventeenth century.

Aristotelian motion, in the first place, carries pervasive connotations of completion, wholeness, and satisfaction. When something moves naturally, for Aristotle, it does so because it is attaining its natural essence — its essential 'whatness'; it is becoming what it truly is, what it is intended to be. In a word, motion is a sort of fulfillment. 'Motion, we say, is the fulfillment of the movable insofar as it is movable.'[12]

Aristotelian movement is teleological. It is caused by attraction toward an end, a purpose, a goal. In seeking to understand a movement, one must consider the final cause, 'that for the sake of which' a thing is done. The *Metaphysics* refers to 'the purpose and the good' as 'the end of all generation and change.'[13] Consequently, Aristotle believed that the nature of a particular movement is determined by its intended destination. To identify a movement or change as being of a particular kind, the crucial consideration is the *telos*, not the immediate or efficient cause. 'It is the goal rather than the starting point of motion that gives its name to a particular process of change.'[14]

From the conception of movement as the actualization of potential, the reaching of an appointed goal, it becomes apparent that Aristotelian movement is a result of a basic tension. Movement is caused by the tension of actual and potential, of essence and existence, of wholeness and incompleteness. This tension, then, a feature of the basic model of motion for Aristotle, is a characteristic of the entire classical universe, and the loss of this tension in the Hobbesian motion-model entails broad and sweeping transformations.

The expression of the tension within a particular organism or substance is an innate striving to attain completion. The inhabitants of Aristotle's universe possess a desire to become what they really and essentially are. This striving is represented by the theory of 'natural tendency' (*hormē*). Everything that moves naturally moves because it is striving—i.e., has a distinctive natural tendency—to act in a certain proper way. A dog has a natural tendency to bark, a stone to fall, and a man, says Aristotle, to seek knowledge. This basic model of striving to attain fulfillment and overcome the tension between potential and actual is applicable to different types of motion, moreover. The model may be basically organic, but it is extended to include human and physical phenomena as well. And in its various manifestations, this reference to *hormē* served Aristotle and the Scholastics as a principle of explanation. Gravitational force was explained therefore by the desire of earth to find its 'proper place', just as the existence of the polis was explained by man's social nature. The motive force of acceleration observed in falling bodies could be attributed by some Scholastics, applying the same principle, to the 'jubilation' of the falling bodies as they neared their 'proper place.'

In the Aristotelian concept of movement inertia was equated with rest. It was always movement and not the lack of movement or the ending of a movement that required explanation. No external principle or force was considered necessary to account for the cessation of movement, for movement was expected to terminate itself by completing the actualization of that which was moved. A physical object was thought to come to rest of itself when it arrived at its proper place, for there was no reason left for it to move. When the final cause was eliminated through fulfillment, one of the necessary conditions of movement was eliminated, and therefore it was entirely natural for the movement to cease. Rest, for Aristotle, is the contrary to motion, 'for rest is the privation of motion and the privation of anything may be called its contrary.'[15] In other words, according to Aristotle, something moves only under the application of some external force, such as the influence of a final cause. If the outside force is removed, then the moving body must come to rest—i.e., to a stop. It was wholly inconceivable to Aristotle and the Aristotelian Scholastics that anything should move unless under force. A constant force, for them, meant constant motion, not constant acceleration.

This equation of inertia with rest became an extraordinarily important interpretative principle when analytically deployed to interpret particular events or actions. Given the Aristotelian doctrine of inertia, it followed that all motion must involve agency, or as Aristotle says, 'everything that is in motion must be moved by something.'[16] Since motion as the mere persistence of a body in a movement which originated from a force no longer present was not conceivable, all movement implied the presence of some sort of guiding force or aspirant desire. This element of active, 'intelligent' guidance was one essential component in any explanation of movement. 'A universe constructed on the mechanics of Aristotle had the door half-way open for spirits already; it was a universe in which unseen hands had to be in constant operation, and sublime Intelligences had to roll the planetary spheres around. Alternatively, bodies had to be endowed with souls and aspirations, so that matter itself seemed to possess mystical qualities.'[17]

This model of movement, with its whole congeries of implications as to teleology, inertia, and tension, was taken over virtually intact and incorporated into the speculations and analyses of medieval scholasticism. The influence of the Aristotelian paradigm of motion is vividly reflected in the formulations of Thomas Aquinas, who was the principal vehicle for the entrenchment of Aristotelian concepts in later medieval philosophy. Aquinas's account of motion is pure Aristotle, plus a little holy water: 'Everything moved, as such, tends as towards a divine likeness, to be perfect in itself; and since a thing is perfect in so far as it becomes actual, it follows that the intention of everything that is in potentiality is to tend to actuality by way of movement.'[18]

This impressive conceptual framework concerning the

phenomenon of motion was totally abandoned as a piece of un-intelligible and obscurantist nonsense by the principal thinkers of the seventeenth century. Its rejection stemmed from a fatal blow in its Achilles heel, its theory of the motion of projectiles and falling bodies. The Aristotelian explanation of projectiles and falling bodies had to remain consistent with the idea that motion always involved a contiguous source of impetus, and it therefore used the 'rush of air' hypothesis. The original source of motion of the projectile was said to have imparted the power of being a 'movent' to the medium in which the projectile was traveling, and the motive power was seen as consecutively transmitted during the projectile's flight. The motion finally stopped 'when one member no longer caused the next member to be a movent but only caused it to be in motion. The motion of these last two,' continues Aristotle, 'must cease simultaneously, and with this the whole motion ceases.'[19] The corresponding theory of falling objects explained the accelera-tion of these bodies as a result of the increasing weight of air above them.

The various difficulties with these accounts had inspired considerable controversy from the fourteenth century on-wards,[20] but these difficulties had never led to the abandon-ment of the basic model, since no substitute model had been developed which could compel widespread acceptance. Alterna-tive theories were developed, but none of them were deemed sufficiently superior to the Aristotelian theory to outweigh the analytical scope and power which the latter possessed. The Aristotelian model of motion continued to prevail into the seventeenth century, therefore, even if its acceptance was somewhat uneasy.[21]

The guiding genius and principal agent in the development of the new view of motion which sparked the seventeenth-century intellectual revolution was Galileo. His decisive conceptual breakthrough was produced by his famous thought experiments, and it had two essential components. First, it involved the transposition of the problem of motion into the abstract world of geometry; and second, it involved the assumption that bodies would continue to move in a straight line unless deflected by an outside source. This combination of a geometricizing method and a new model of inertia proved to be such a potent source of simple and lucid theoretical explanation that it quickly dominated the minds of the leading intellectuals of the seventeenth century.

Descartes offers a profound example of this impact. For the new consciousness which he represents, the Aristotelian account of motion was completely useless. The transformation was so total and unqualified that the abstract spatial—i.e., geometrical—idea of motion, an idea quite foreign to centuries of scholars, catapulted into the charmed circle of Descartes's clear and distinct ideas. 'The learned,' complains Descartes, 'have a way of being so clever as to continue to render themselves blind to things that are in their own nature evident.'[22] The case of motion is the outstanding example of this blindness, Descartes says: 'They define *motion*, a fact with which everyone is quite familiar, as "the actualization of what exists in potentiality, in so far as it is potential!" Now who understands these words? And who at the same time does not know what motion is? Will not everyone admit that those philosophers have been trying to find a knot in a bulrush?'[23]

Hobbes was of like mind. In fact, he went further than the somewhat more conservative Descartes, who freed such spiritual concepts as 'mind', 'soul', and 'God' from the confines of mechanical motion by assigning them a separate realm. Hobbes was a resolute monist who saw motion as comprising the whole of reality. As a result, Hobbes's acceptance of the motion model had more far-reaching implications, extending into his anthropology and political thought, than the similar acceptance by Descartes. The problems of a dualist like Descartes were to be found in epistemology, where the dualism had to be surmounted, while the problems of the monistic Hobbes arose from the attempt to compress the whole universe into the confines of his monism. Similarly, the monistic

Spinoza's entire world view was influenced far more profoundly by his hypostasization of the new view of inertia in his
conatus sese conservandi, than was the world view of Descartes.
Descartes, in fact, did not concern himself extensively with a
weltanschauung; for him, geometry was a method more than
an ontology.

For Hobbes, however, the geometricization of movement was
not simply an approach to certain problems, but was also a
revelation of the nature of the universe itself. He saw geometry
not as an abstract, formal science, but as a revelation of the
form of motion.[24] In his view, Galileo had not simply provided
the basis for a science of mechanics, but had produced the
foundation of an entire cosmology. The task he took upon
himself was the elaboration of the motion model into a complete
natural philosophy. In his dedicatory epistle to *De Corpore*
Hobbes explicitly states the possibility of developing this new
natural philosophy and acknowledges his indebtedness to
Galileo. 'Galileus in our time . . . was the first that opened to
us the gate of natural philosophy universal, which is the
knowledge of the nature of *motion*. So that neither can the age
of natural philosophy be reckoned higher than to him.'[25]

This belief that motion holds the key to nature, a conviction
which is both methodological and ontological, is not novel.
It is important to realize that Hobbes is here actually following
the lead of Aristotle, who also saw the knowledge of the nature
of motion to be the 'gate of natural philosophy.' Aristotle's
expression of this proposition is as follows: 'Nature has been
defined as a principle of motion and change, and it is the
subject of our inquiry. We must therefore see that we understand the meaning of motion; for if it were unknown, the
meaning of "nature" too would be unknown.'[26] In keeping
with our basic analysis of the pattern of tacit-framework-
persistence and explicit-model-replacement in the shift from
Aristotle to Hobbes, then, it is possible to say that Hobbes
insists upon the profound ramifications of the new model of
motion precisely because he is, formally speaking, a good

Aristotelian, even while he is jettisoning Aristotle's view of what motion is.

To begin his natural philosophy, then, Hobbes, like Aristotle, begins with the study of motion. But whereas Aristotle had turned principally to biological growth and human deeds Hobbes turns to geometry to find this crucial knowledge: 'and such writers or disputes thereof, as are ignorant of geometry, do but make their readers and hearers lose their time'.[27] The nature of motion which geometry reveals, says Hobbes, is 'nothing but change of place.'[28] Moreover, Hobbes asserts that 'all mutation consists in motion.'[29] Together, these two basic assumptions make up the proposition that Hobbes tries to maintain throughout his consideration of everything from physics to politics: all change is really nothing but change of place. To complete the chain of definition, it should be noted that 'place' for Hobbes has none of the warm and amiable characteristics that it sometimes had for Aristotle—e.g., in the concept of 'natural place.' Aristotelian 'place' had 'homes' in it, but Hobbesian 'place' is an empty geometrical abstraction.

The 'motion' which Hobbes sees as the very life of the universe is far different from Aristotle's 'movement.' Where Aristotelian movement was finite, Hobbesian movement is infinite. It has no order, no structure, no end or limitation. It is endless, aimless motion. It is not 'from . . . to . . . ,' as Aristotle assumed, but rather an endless chain without a goal. Hobbes therefore deletes from change the connotation of fulfillment which formed a part of Aristotle's definition of motion as the actualization of potential. 'Potentiality' Hobbes consigns to oblivion as another vain and empty phrase of the Scholastics. As he says in his *Answer to Bishop Bramhall*: 'There is no such word as potentiality in the Scriptures, nor in any author of the Latin tongue. It is found only in School-divinity, as a word of art, or rather as a word of craft, to amaze and puzzle the laity.'[30]

The pervasive teleological character of motion in the Aristotelian-Scholastic model, therefore, disappears completely in the Hobbesian model. End-less motion is, by definition, motion without a *telos*. This disappearance of teleology from the Hobbesian universe is seen in Hobbes's discussion of causation.

All causes are motions for Hobbes. 'Universal things,' he tells us, 'have all but one universal cause, which is motion . . . and motion cannot be understood to have any other cause besides motion.'[31] The Aristotelian understanding of causation as a complex of material, efficient, formal, and final elements is therefore dispensable, and causation becomes a sort of constant succession, like the transmission of momentum along a row of billiard balls. Efficient cause, seen as momentum, subsumes the Aristotelian formal and final causes, which thereby lose their previous force. 'The writers of metaphysics reckon up two other causes besides the efficient and material, namely the essence, which some call the formal cause, and the end, or final cause; both which are nevertheless efficient causes.'[32]

The consequences of this conceptual transformation are radical and far-reaching. As Brandt says, these lines consigning final causes to the trash bin 'must have had the effect of the blow of a bludgeon on Hobbes's Aristotelian contemporaries. A whole world perished with the giving up of the final causes.'[33]

For Aristotle, force exerted by a contiguous agent was necessary for any movement. This was the efficient cause. But the force of this contiguous agent was not in itself a sufficient explanation of movement. On the contrary, it was the final cause or *telos* which was not only necessary, but was pre-eminent; the name of a movement came from its goal. When defining or characterizing a specific movement, Aristotle looked first to 'that for the sake of which.' Hobbes quite emphatically abandons this view and asserts that the force of a contiguous body is entirely sufficient to explain any motion; in fact, there is no other cause to consider. 'There can be no cause of motion,' he says, 'except in a body contiguous and moved.' He continues:

For let there be any two bodies which are not contiguous, and betwixt which the intermediate space is empty, or, if filled, filled with another body which is at rest; and let one of the propounded leaders be supposed to be at rest; I say it shall always be at rest. For if it shall be moved, the cause of that motion . . . will be some external body; and therefore, if between it and that external body there be nothing but empty space, then whatsoever the disposition be of that external body or of the patient itself, yet if it be supposed to be now at rest, we may conceive it will continue so till it be touched by some other body.[34]

The notion of 'agency' is therefore reduced by Hobbes to merely 'the aggregate of all such accidents,'[35] that is, the sum total of external forces exerted by bodies 'contiguous and moved.'

The same principle, Hobbes says, is seen in the new doctrine of inertia:

The same reason may serve to prove that whatsoever is moved, will always be moved on in the same way and with the same velocity, except it be hindered by some other contiguous and moved body; and consequently that no bodies, either when they are at rest, or when there is an interposition of vacuum, can generate or extinguish or lessen motion in other bodies. There is one that has written that things moved are more resisted by things at rest, than by things contrarily moved; for this reason, that he conceived motion not to be so contrary to motion as rest. That which deceived him was, that the words *rest* and *motion* are but contradictory names; whereas motion, indeed, is not resisted by rest, but by contrary motion.[36]

There really is no such thing as 'rest' for Hobbes; there are only motions and contrary motions. This viewpoint marked a decisive shift from the Aristotelian idea. Rest for Aristotle

E

enjoyed an ontological primacy; rest was the repose of something that had reached its end or fulfillment. Rest was a mark of wholeness and completion, a completion toward which all motion was striving. In a sense, then, rest was really the 'cause' of movement, a source of impetus. Motion was a function of rest, and this relationship par excellence symbolized the finitude of the universe.

Hobbes sees no impetus in rest; impetus resides only in a body contiguous and moved. In effect, then, he abolishes rest in the Aristotelian sense altogether. His world is 'rest-less.' The only use he gives rest is to signify a basically accidental absence of motion. The Hobbesian position, in short, is a fully conscious elaboration of the new idea of inertia. Whereas Aristotle and the Thomists, beginning with the ontological primacy of rest, saw movements as problematic departures from this state, Hobbes makes rest merely one possible configuration of motion, qualitatively no different from any other vector of forces. Rest is no longer peculiarly natural. A body at rest is no different, except accidentally, from an unopposed body continuing its motion indefinitely in the same direction. Rest in the Aristotelian sense of absence of movement is no longer primary, but merely one possible type of unaccelerated motion, which is now given ontological primacy. The Aristotelian cosmology revolved around the distinction between movement and rest; the new distinction is between continuous motion and acceleration, and the Aristotelian distinction is rendered inconsequential and meaningless.

The obliteration of the Aristotelian distinction and the substitution of the new distinction, the replacement of the ontological primacy of rest by the ontological primacy of sustained motion, brings with it a transformation in the whole root conception of change. No longer does movement imply tension. Natural movement is no longer a striving to attain, but rather a simple continuation. The direction of a motion is not formal and substantive, but vectorial. Movement is not structured by a goal, but is wholly guided by a preceding concatenation of motions. The basic characteristic of motion, therefore, is not to grow, or develop, or reach fulfillment, but to persist, to continue *ad infinitum*. Any modification of an original force is a deflection, not a maturity.

Finally, motion is homogeneous for Hobbes. He regards all movements as simply one form or another of simple change of place. Therefore, the Aristotelian distinction between natural and violent motion disappears. In a sense, both are absorbed, and hence dissolved, under the principle of necessity which for Hobbes encompasses the universe. All the motions in Hobbes's world form a conceptual amalgam that corresponds rather closely to the Aristotelian conception of spontaneity or chance, i.e., incidental motions, which would by definition be contrary to nature in things which had a natural motion. (Natural, in this context, means for Aristotle, for its given purpose; the whole distinction turns around the notion of teleology.) The Aristotelian term for spontaneity is *to automaton*—things that move for no reason. Hobbesian movement is all 'automatic,' and life itself for Hobbes consists in automaticity. 'Why may we not say,' he asks, 'that all automata (Engines that move themselves by springs and wheeles as doth a watch) have an artificial life?'[37] Aristotle would answer that life involves purposeful striving, as automaticity does not. But Hobbes would consider this objection to be merely a function of the outmoded Aristotelian idea of movement. The Aristotelian distinction between natural and automatic movements had been abandoned by Hobbes with the abandonment of the dichotomy between rest and movement. Violent motion for Hobbes is accelerated motion, and the distinction between natural and automatic motion is no longer involved in any natural/violent motion distinction, but can rather be resolved in favor of automaticity. Natural movements are automatic for Hobbes.

Just as Aristotle applied his potency/actuality model of movement, based on the conception of inertia as rest, to all types of natural movements, whether they be physical, biological, or human, Hobbes applied his idea of motion, the purposeless, automatic preservation of an original impetus, to all types of movements. In the finite cosmos of Aristotle and the Thomists, 'everything that comes to be moves toward an end';[38] in the Hobbesian world everything that comes to be moves *ad infinitum*. Motion reigns throughout the entire phenomenal universe, which for Hobbes unlike Descartes is the whole of reality. When Descartes geometricized motion, he removed himself and God from this mechanism, and philosophers began to puzzle over the connection between these 'ghosts' and the machine of the world. However anti-Scholastic Hobbes may be, he shared the characteristic Aristotelian rejection of all such dualisms. The unified world view of Aristotle suited his resolutely monistic sensibility very well, once he transformed the 'obscurantist' idea of movement into his 'clear' idea of motion. As J. H. Randall observed in his book *Aristotle*, 'in many fundamental respects, Hobbes remained a good Ockhamite Aristotelian.'[39]

Hobbes undertook the universal transformation of movement into motion with a methodical thoroughness. He felt motion to be the basic principle not merely of physical bodies, but of all the constituents of the universe, including nature, life, and mind. That is, having developed and articulated his basic model of motion, Hobbes applies it systematically to the entire furniture of the cosmos. This universal application of a root-paradigm is a step which once more was prefigured, hence invited, by Aristotelian cosmology. Aristotle, too, applied his own paradigm of motion to all realms of reality: physical, biological, and human. The formal patterns of Hobbes's cosmology are, therefore, once more taken as prefabricated from the structure of the Aristotelian framework. The only differences, albeit crucial ones, are in the nature of the explicit model being used and the direction of its movement from one cosmological level to another. The explicit Aristotelian model is finite and teleological, the Hobbesian counterpart is infinite and inertial. The Aristotelian model is basically biological in origin and transported from there into the physical and political realms; the Hobbesian model originates in the interpretation of physical events and is thence exported into biological and social analyses.

The first critical step that Hobbes takes in his transposition of the motion model from the realm of physical motion to the whole of reality appears with his concept of 'vital motion.' Living bodies, of course, move, but is it possible to conceive of their movements as another species of inertial motion? Hobbes was convinced that they could be so conceived. His immediate inspiration with regard to this question was the work of William Harvey, who made his discovery of the principle of circulation almost wholly on the basis of arithmetic calculations. Harvey's methods were instinctively appealing to Hobbes, who was convinced that geometric tools provided the only effectual means for understanding anything that moved. Proceeding on this basis, Harvey considered the physiological functions of the circulatory system as a mechanical system. He spoke of the heart, for example, as 'a piece of machinery in which though one wheel gives motion to another, yet all the wheels seem to move simultaneously.'

Seizing this image of the mechanism of circulation, Hobbes identifies it with the principle of life itself. Circulation is 'vital motion.' 'Now vital motion is the motion of the blood, perpetually circulating (as hath been shown from many infallible signs and marks by Doctor Harvey the first observer of it) in the veins and arteries.'[40] It is difficult to overemphasize the significance of the interpretative leap which Hobbes makes here. By identifying vitality, or life in its biological aspect, with the motion of the circulatory system, Hobbes converts vitality into a mechanism. The perpetually circulating blood, which is a kind of circular inertial system, becomes life itself. The 'original of life,' as Hobbes says, is 'in the heart,'[41] which has been identified as a mechanical pump. Consequently, it is possible to say, as Hobbes does, that life is 'but a motion of limbs.'[42]

Inertial motion, by definition, involves a tendency to persist in its movement. Hobbes uses this aspect of his motion model, then, to extend it to the more complex manifestations of life, such as the will and the passions of living creatures. Life is motion, says Hobbes; this much is established. Motion tends to persist, and this tendency constitutes the striving of the organism.

> But if vital motion be helped by motion made by sense, then the parts of the organ will be disposed to guide the spirits in such manner as conduceth most to the preservation and augmentation of that motion, by the help of the nerves. And in animal motion this is the very first endeavour, and found even in the embryo; which while it is in the womb, moveth its limbs with voluntary motion, for the avoiding of whatsoever troubleth it, or for the pursuing of what pleaseth it. And this first endeavour, when it tends towards such things as are known by experience to be pleasant, is called *appetite*, that is, an approaching; and when it shuns what is troublesome, *aversion*, or flying from it.[43]

Once again an established Aristotelian concept—in this instance, that of *hormē*—has been transformed. Like Aristotle, Hobbes sees organisms as characterized by natural tendencies, by inherent strivings; but this is the striving to persist, not the desire to reach a *telos*. The central phenomenon of endeavour is, in Hobbes's view, a kind of biological inertia, an in-finitized *hormē*.

The spread of the motion model as the paradigm of all the manifestations of life proceeds next to the will. This step follows quite easily, for Hobbes sees the will as essentially identical with appetite.[44] The only reason for their having different names, Hobbes says, is that will is appetite which succeeds deliberation. But deliberation effects no real transformation of the appetite before it issues into will; nor in fact could it, for deliberation too is seen by Hobbes on the model of a vector of mechanical motions. Deliberation is, in fact, simply the vicissitude of contending appetites and aversions.[45] Hence, the will is the resultant vector which emerges from the whole welter of various appetites. And since the will is one species of appetite, it too is a species of motion, for the appetites and aversions are 'motions of the heart.'[46]

Not only are the passions motions, in Hobbes's view, but cognition also can be conceived as a form of motion. That is, the intellectual faculties as well as the emotional strivings of living creatures are, at bottom, nothing but motion. The reduction of cognition to motion is mediated in Hobbes's system through the pivotal concept of sensation. The problem of sensation was a principal focus in the 'Little Treatise' in 1630, and it remained central in Hobbes's mind throughout his philosophical speculations. (The first chapter of the *Leviathan*, for example, is entitled 'Of Sense.') Again, this approach to the phenomenon of cognition through an examination of sensation is patterned after Aristotle, whose epistemological reflections proceed in the same way.[47]

The Aristotelian tradition made the senses the basic organs of the understanding. Nothing was held to be in the mind that was not previously in the senses. The senses, moreover, were trusted as a source of knowledge; what they revealed to the mind were genuine aspects of external reality. If the mind saw colors, then colors were sensible qualities, features of the real world.

In the Cartesian version of the seventeenth-century intellectual revolution, the Aristotelian view of sensation is doubly challenged. Both the unavoidable reliance of the mind upon the senses and the essential trustworthiness of the senses are denied by Descartes. Descartes began his epistemology from a stance of radical distrust of the senses. This distrust, in fact, was the real substance of the famed Cartesian doubt. The senses, he felt, had led men into gross errors in their search for knowledge; therefore, the senses had to be circumvented. As Descartes put it in his first Meditation: 'All that up to the present time I have accepted as most true and certain I have learned either from the senses or through the senses; but it is sometimes proved to me that these senses are deceptive, and it is wiser not to trust entirely to any thing by which we have once been deceived.'[48]

Descartes's solution to the unreliability of the senses was neo-Platonic. He felt that it is possible to rely upon intuition, which can give knowledge of clear and distinct ideas that are not contingent upon sensation. Mathematical ideas are of this class and so are the ideas of God and the soul. Descartes felt certain that these ideas do not come from the senses. 'Even the philosophers in the Schools hold it as a maxim that there is nothing in the understanding which has not first of all been in the senses, *in which there is certainly no doubt that the ideas of God and of the soul have never been.*'[49] In other words, one challenge to the Aristotelian account of sensation served to save Descartes from the potentially disastrous consequences of the other challenge. The possible dangers of the unreliability of the senses are staved off by the denial that we have only the senses to rely upon as a source of knowledge. By making important areas of knowledge 'angelic,' Descartes can circumvent the unreliable senses.

Hobbes's notion of senses is rather curious, but important. He, like Descartes, knows the senses to be deceptive, but he will have none of the Cartesian mysticism of mental powers detached from the senses. He retains the Aristotelian–Scholastic conjunction of the mind with the senses: 'For there is no conception in a man's mind, which hath not at first, totally, or by parts, been begotten upon the organs of Sense.'[50] Rather than separate the mind from the senses and give greater reliance to the former, as Descartes does, Hobbes transforms the senses into a species of motion and then extends this model into the mind. Sensible qualities, which Aristotle and the Scholastics considered to be qualities of the object of sense, are removed from the world by Hobbes. What really is there as the cause of sensation is the motion of the object; the colors, sounds, and odors are 'apparitions.' 'Whatsoever accidents or qualities our senses make us think there be in the world, they be not there, but are seeming and apparition only: the things that really are in the world without us, are those motions by which these seemings are caused.'[51] If sensible qualities are not in the object, though, they are not in us either. 'Neither in us that are pressed, are they anything else but divers motions.'[52]

This formulation leaves Hobbes with some insuperable difficulties. For one thing, by rejecting the nonsensible perceptions of Descartes he leaves himself dependent upon the very senses which he knows to be potentially deceptive. Moreover, he never provides any satisfactory account of the nature or the location of the 'apparitions' or 'fancies' at all. They are not in the object, but they are not in the mind either.[53] Nevertheless, whatever its inherent difficulties, this formulation enables Hobbes to achieve his intended goal, namely, the reduction of knowledge as well as the passions to a form of motion.

The reduction of knowledge to motion is accomplished through the following equations. There are two kinds of knowledge, and 'both of these sorts are but experience.'[54] But all experience is memory, and hence knowledge is just memory. 'All experience being, as I have said, but remembrance, all knowledge is remembrance.'[55] Memory is the same as imagination. 'Imagination and Memory, are but one thing, which for divers considerations hath divers names.'[56] But 'imagination . . . is nothing but decaying sense.'[57] And because sense is nothing but 'divers motion,' the chain of reductive equations is completed, and all knowledge becomes motion.

Such, then, is the nature and the scope of the new concept of motion which played on Hobbes's imagination and thenceforth served him as an analytical paradigm of universal applicability. In Hobbes's world the Aristotelian configuration of purposeful, finite movements had disappeared entirely. In their stead remained a homogeneous swarm of incoherent, aimless perpetuations of momentum that had no capacity for growth, for fulfillment, or for rest. The new universe was open-ended rather than finite, literally restless, and completely without intrinsic ordering purposes beyond the striving to persist in its motion.

NOTES

1. *The Origins of Modern Science* (New York: Collier Books, 1962), p. 15.
2. Norwood Hanson examines the role of such shifts of perceptual gestalt in scientific understanding in his *Patterns of Discovery* (Cambridge, Eng., Cambridge University Press, 1958).
3. Butterfield, *The Origins of Modern Science*, p. 19.
4. Peters, *Hobbes*, p. 85.
5. *Leviathan*, p. 8.
6. Peters, *Hobbes*, p. 94. See also Brandt's observation that 'the whole of his philosophy is built up on the foundation of one single, quite simple idea, the idea of motion' (Brandt, *Thomas Hobbes's Mechanical Conception of Nature*, p. 379).
7. Aristotle, *Metaphysics*, 1. 9. 991b.
8. *Metaphysics*, 7. 11. 1037a.
9. Aristotle, *Physics*, 5. 2. 225b.
10. *Physics*, 5. 1. 225a.
11. *Physics*, 3. 1. 200b.
12. Aristotle, *Physics*, 8. 1. 251a.
13. Aristotle, *Metaphysics*, 1. 3. 983a.
14. Aristotle, *Physics*, 5. 1. 224b.
15. Aristotle, *Physics*, 5. 6. 229b.
16. Aristotle, *Physics*, 7. 1. 241b.
17. Butterfield, *The Origins of Modern Science*, p. 19.
18. Thomas Aquinas, *Summa Contra Gentiles*, 3: 22.
19. Aristotle, *Physics*, 8. 10. 267a.
20. See Herbert Butterfield, *The Origins of Modern Science*, chapt. 1.
21. This pattern is in keeping with Kuhn's generalization that

'the decision to reject one paradigm is always simultaneously the decision to accept another.' Kuhn, *Structure of Scientific Revolutions*, p. 77.

22. Rene Descartes, *Rules for the Direction of the Mind*, trans. E. S. Haldane and G. R. T. Ross, Great Books Series, Vol. 31 (Chicago: University of Chicago Press, 1952), p. 23.

23. Ibid., p. 24.

24. As Peters says, he 'made geometry a particular branch of kinematics' (Peters, *Hobbes*, p. 87).

25. Hobbes, *English Works*, 1: viii.

26. Aristotle, *Physics*, 3. 1. 200b.

27. Hobbes, *English Works*, 1: 73.

28. Ibid., 7: 83–4.

29. Ibid., 1: 70.

30. Ibid., 4: 299.

31. Ibid., 1: 69–70.

32. Ibid., 1: 131.

33. *Thomas Hobbes's Mechanical Conception of Nature*, p. 290.

34. Hobbes, *English Works*, 1: 124.

35. Ibid., p. 125

36. Ibid.

37. Hobbes, *Leviathan*, p. 3.

38. Aristotle, *Metaphysics*, 9. 8. 1050a.

39. (New York: Columbia University Press, 1960), p. 72.

40. Hobbes, *English Works*, 1: 407.

41. Ibid., p. 406.

42. *Leviathan*, p. 3.

43. Hobbes, *English Works*, 1: 407.

44. 'The same thing is called both will and appetite.' Hobbes, *English Works*, 1: 409.

45. Ibid., p. 408.

46. Ibid., p. 401.

47. For a careful demonstration of the parallelisms of Hobbes and Aristotle at this point, see Brandt, *Thomas Hobbes's Mechanical Conception of Nature*, chapt. 1.

48. Rene Descartes, *Meditations*, trans. E. S. Haldane and

G. R. T. Ross, Great Books Series, Vol. 31 (Chicago: University of Chicago Press, 1952), p. 75.

49. Rene Descartes, *Discourse on Method*, trans. E. S. Haldane and G. R. T. Ross, Great Books Series, Vol. 31 (Chicago: University of Chicago Press, 1952), p. 53.

50. Hobbes, *Leviathan*, p. 7.

51. Hobbes, *English Works*, 1: 8.

52. Hobbes, *Leviathan*, p. 8.

53. 'The result one must educe from his exposition is: The sensible qualities are neither objective nor subjective' (Brandt, *Thomas Hobbes's Mechanical Conception of Nature*, p. 40).

54. Hobbes, *English Works*, 4: 27.

55. Ibid.

56. Hobbes, *Leviathan*, p. 11.

57. Ibid., p. 10.

3

The Corporealization of Substance

'Substance is the starting point of everything.' — *Aristotle*

'Substance and Body signifie the same thing.' — *Hobbes*

The Aristotelian cosmos was composed of substance and movement. The notion of 'substance' was the correlate of 'movement', for it was within substance that movement occurred, connecting the potential and the completed actuality. The Hobbesian universe is composed, in contrast but in parallel, of motion and 'body', ideas as closely interconnected as substance and movement. The rejection of one member of each pair involves the corresponding rejection of the other member. Therefore, the results of Hobbes's disavowal of movement was a parallel disavowal of substance, and vice versa. The Aristotelian rubric of substance/movement remains as a form in Hobbes's body/motion, but the content is no longer there. Part of Hobbes's transformation of the classical cosmos, it can literally be said, involved draining the universe of its 'substance.'

Aristotle's concept of 'ousia' is very difficult to understand. The noted Aristotle scholar W. D. Ross, for example, termed Aristotle's principal treatment of 'ousia', the *Metaphysics*, a 'desperately difficult' work. Not only do textual and philological problems impede our understanding of Aristotle, but many knowledgeable scholars believe that Aristotle himself, using the concept heuristically as much as purely denotatively, was not fully clear in his own mind concerning 'ousia.'[1] The apparent inconsistencies and virtually irreconcilable uses of the term in the Aristotelian corpus make it possible to refute almost any general interpretation a commentator might suggest. The tendency is to read into the text one's own presuppositions, since there is sufficient leeway to do so if the commentator takes some liberties with the text. In spite of all these difficulties and temptations, however, a few general statements about the functioning of the notion of 'ousia' in Aristotle must be risked if the impact and full meaning of Hobbes's parallel concept of body are to be appreciated.

The most striking feature of the concept of 'ousia' in Aristotle is its omnipresence. Just as Hobbes felt that 'every part of the universe is body,' Aristotle felt that every thing in the universe was substance.[2] 'As in syllogisms, substance is the starting point of everything.'[3] Everything that can be said to be at all has its being by virtue of its relation to substance. 'We have treated of that which is primarily and to which all the other categories of being are referred—i.e.—of substance. For it is in virtue of the concept of substance that the others also are said to be.'[4] The substance of something is simply that by which it is what it is—its formula, its identity, its essential whatness. In Aristotle's view, to define anything was to give an account of its substance, and conversely the substance of an entity was equivalent to its essential definition. Morphologically, 'ousia' was formed from the feminine singular of the present participle of the verb 'to be.'[5] Linguistically, the concept of 'ousia' was the transmutation into a noun form of the verb which indicated simple existence, and the philosophical realism of Aristotle was based partly upon the attribution of ontological significance to this linguistic form.

Obviously, as Aristotle took great pains to point out, there are many different kinds of substance just as there are many different uses of the verb 'to be.' Much of the Aristotelian corpus, in fact, consists of a bewildering array of distinctions among the various kinds of substance and among the different meanings of that term which Aristotle perceived. Some substances are primary, some not.[6] Some substances are perceptible, some intelligible but not perceptible.[7] Substance 'is of two kinds, the concrete thing and the formula,'[8] with the former capable of destruction while the latter is not. Substance is not a universal,[9] but it is nevertheless separable from matter, at least in principle.[10] Since some of these distinctions and the implications that should follow from them are not maintained consistently, moreover, it becomes extremely difficult to know precisely what Aristotle did mean substance to be in any general sense. Perhaps the simplest explanation he gives is his statement that substance is 'what makes this thing flesh and that a syllable.'[11] And that which makes something what it is is basically its 'indwelling form.'[12]

Relative to the radical reformulation that the problem underlying the concept of substance (i.e., what is it that maintains identity through change?) received in the seventeenth century, two characteristics of the Aristotelian notion of 'ousia' are especially important. The first characteristic is the incredible breadth of the single concept and, consequently, the great burden which it carried in the system as a whole. Through its application to a vast array of disparate phenomena, 'ousia' represented an attempt to encompass within a single format the entire realm of being. Everything that existed in the realm of nature—i.e., the ordered world—took its place within the bounds of a particular substance from which its own individual existence was derived. Despite Aristotle's generally keen eye for subtle distinctions, his application of this common format across the different realms of being—the physical, the biological, the conscious—tended to blur the important differences among them. The capstone of the Aristotelian imposition of a homogeneous format upon heterogeneous subject matter was his concept of 'nature,' which will be examined more carefully in the following chapter. The common format provided by the universal application of the concept of 'ousia' permitted the use of central concepts such as desire, natural tendency, rest, purpose, and end throughout the *Physics* as well as *De Anima*. The continuity of all the orders of being was emphasized. The human, the biological, and the physical were all 'substantial' and hence subject to a basically similar set of ground rules.

The concept of 'ousia,' then, represented the common principles of finitude and coherence which together characterized the Aristotelian natural cosmos. The concept, therefore, carried a great burden and has been subject to various interpretations. Functionalists have found that the notion of 'ousia' was in many uses a functional and dynamic concept; medieval theologians applied 'ousia' to the divine activity of God; leading seventeenth-century thinkers found 'ousia' to be 'substance' in the material, atomistic sense that the word has come to have in modern times. In a sense, all these interpretations are right. The naturalist interpretation is right in that Aristotle saw the natural elements and certain physical properties as 'ousiae.'[13] The functionalist interpretation is right in that 'ousiae' were often defined in terms of process, as for example in the discussion of the faculties of the soul.[14] The theological interpretation is right in that the completion of the defining movement of an 'ousia'—i.e., a movement in which the end is present—was considered an activity.[15]

That each of the above interpretations has some validity is perhaps not as significant as the fact that all of them are to some extent valid. The partial validity of all the interpretations reflects the role of the concept of 'ousia' as a framework within which disparate phenomena are given common principles of existence. In effect, the status of 'ousia' could be given to anything that could be put into the form of an irreducible noun— i.e., a noun that cannot be resolved without destroying its essential whatness. As a result, the brace of 'ousiae,' within which movements occurred and which together made up the realm of Aristotelian nature, extended as a continuum from the lowest substance to the divine substance. In the application of this common framework, the lower end of the continuum became somewhat overendowed while the upper end became relatively impoverished. Thus the elements themselves took on aspects of desire and purposiveness, while Aristotle's treatment of human emotions was often rather wooden.[16] Taken simply as an analogical principle of ultimate similarity, which was one of its central roles within the Aristotelian system, the concept of 'ousia' provided a channel through which characteristics of one realm of being could pervade another realm. As long as the general direction of flow was from anthropomorphic regions into the physical realm, political speculation could be reasonably healthy at the expense of failures in the physical disciplines. When the direction was reversed, however, the health of physics was purchased at the expense of political sanity by those who, like Hobbes, maintained the fundamental Aristotelian analogy throughout the realms of being.

The second characteristic of the Aristotelian concept of 'ousia' important for grasping its dissolution in the seventeenth century is its incipient materialism. By materialism in this context is not meant the crude atomism of Democritus or the spatialism of the seventeenth century, but rather a congeries of attributes which suggest a root intellectual model that sees the world in terms of *things*. This model is a spatial model, though not in the seventeenth-century sense of space since Aristotelian space is impregnated with sensibility and perfectibility. Being was characterized by finitude and by a human, valuational content of location. Human purposes and attributes were 'placed,' opening the way for the comfortable 'interpenetration of space and destiny' that characterized Scholastic theology, based as it was on Aristotelian notions.

Part of this peculiarly Aristotelian incipient materialism was linguistic in origin. The Stagirite's relentless quest for the basic principles of Being was essentially noun-oriented. As the primary data of reality, Aristotle took 'ness-es' instead of 'ings,' subjects and predicates instead of verbs. Before attempting to investigate the nature of anything, he almost invariably converted it into a noun form. Even the central concept of 'ousia' is the transposition of the most simple verb, 'to be,' into a noun. The objects of inquiry, then, were almost always 'ness-es' and things, 'properties,' 'parts,' and 'accidents.' Whatever was ultimately a subject of predication[17] was seen

F

as ultimately real, and not only real, but impenetrably so. Viewing these ultimate nouns as irreducible categories of being then tended to freeze the lines of reality from which they were drawn, and the consequence was a whole host of philosophical dilemmas that have plagued Aristotle's heirs ever since—e.g., the theological problem of how the divine and human 'ousiae' may be conjoined and the epistemological problem of how subject and object 'ousiae' can meet.

The second strand of Aristotle's incipient materialism was the significance attributed to place. 'Place' was a potent force in the Aristotelian cosmos and was a correlate of the doctrine of rest. Things came to rest when they reached their natural place, and therefore movements could be explained by the attempt to reach these spatial 'homes.' Aristotelian space was heterogeneous and valuational, and these two features were interrelated. *What* something was, its position in the natural order, was related to *where* it was. Myth was woven into cosmology and emotions into motions—hence the 'jubilation' of falling bodies and the perfection of the highest heaven. When the seventeenth-century thinkers homogenized space, they were logically led to homogenize, and consequently destroy, values as well. Hierarchy and order in Being were tied in with hierarchical space and disappeared with it.

Aristotle had no intention of being materialistic in any way. His linguistically induced tendency to view substance as that which made matter into some 'definite thing,'[18] and his basically spatial consciousness were susceptible to materialistic conclusions, however; and, realizing this tendency, Aristotle carefully distinguished his views from explicit materialism. The ultimate foundation of Aristotle's intellectual attack on materialists, however, was his conception of movement which was discarded with the seventeenth-century view of inertia. Aristotle argued that a purely corporeal view of the universe could not explain movement: 'Those, then, who say the universe is one and posit one kind of thing as matter, and as corporeal matter which has spatial magnitude, evidently go astray in many ways. For they posit the elements of bodies only, not of incorporeal things, though there are also incorporeal things. And in trying to state the causes of generation and destruction, and in giving a physical account of all things, they do away with the cause of movement.'[19] Aristotle, therefore, with good reason but nevertheless quite fatally, hinged his conception of 'ousiae' upon his conception of finite teleological movement. When his conception of movement succumbed to the Galilean theory of impetus, the way was cleared for the reduction of substance to mere matter, a reduction contrary to the whole intention of Aristotle's philosophy. Aristotle would have considered such a corporeal universe completely unknowable: 'matter is unknowable in itself.'[20] The generation of Descartes, Hobbes, Galileo, and Mersenne found this to be no problem, for the language of matter and the key to the principles of motion were revealed to them by geometry. The language of numbers superseded the language of nouns, and substance disappeared from the universe.

Whatever the philosophical differences that may have existed among Hobbes's contemporaries, they shared in common a view of substance that was a radical departure from the significance that term held for Aristotle. The problem for which the notion of 'ousia' served as an answer to Aristotle — i.e., what are the finite channels within which movements take place? — no longer bothered them. The new concept of inertia removed the problem for them. Whereas Aristotle saw substances as the stable patterns or entities within which movements took place, the seventeenth-century thinkers saw substances as something very similar to Aristotle's 'material substratum.' The common element in the Aristotelian and seventeenth-century uses of the term is its designation for that which remains stable throughout change, but there is a radical shift in the conception of what does remain unchanging. The retention of a common functional use of the term leads in the new world view to its application to an entirely different referent. In a sense, then, it can be said that the modern meaning of substance is almost diametrically opposite to the meaning it had for Aristotle.[21]

Descartes conceived of two basic substances, mind and body, the former having the power of thought but no extension and the latter having extension but no power of thought. Locke saw substance as an unknowable something that served as an empty vehicle for qualities:

> So that if any one will examine himself concerning the notion of pure substance in general, he will find that he has no other idea of it at all, but only a supposition of he knows not what support of such qualities which are capable of producing simple ideas in us; which qualities are commonly called accidents. If any one should be asked, what is the subject wherein color or weight inheres, he would have nothing to say, but the solid extended parts; and if he were demanded, what is it that solidity and extension inhere in, he would not be in a much better case than the Indian before mentioned, who, saying that the world was supported by a great elephant, was asked what the elephant rested on; to which his answer was — a great tortoise: but being again pressed to know what gave support to the broad-backed tortoise, replied — something, he knew not what.[22]

For Hobbes substance becomes simply that which is extended — 'body,' and the aggregate of bodies comprises the entire universe. 'The word "Body" in the most general acceptation, signifieth that which filleth, or occupyeth some certain room, or imagined place, and dependeth not on the imagination, but is a reall part of what we call the Universe. For the Universe, being the Aggregate of all Bodies, there is no reall part thereof that is not also Body; nor any thing properly A Body, that is not also part of (that Aggregate of all Bodies) the Universe. . . . And according to this acceptation of the word, Substance and Body signify the same thing.'[23]

In arriving at this formulation of the content of the universe, Hobbes is explicitly critical of Aristotelian philosophy and the doctrines of Scholasticism based on Aristotle. Having enumerated what he considers to be some disastrous aspects of this mode of philosophy, he concludes with one of his inimitable diatribes: 'And I believe that scarce anything can be more absurdly said in natural Philosophy, than that which now is called Aristotle's *Metaphysiques*, nor more repugnant to Government, than much of that he hath said in his *Politiques*; nor more ignorantly than a great part of his *Ethiques*.'[24]

The fuming of the old Englishman was not wholly empty irascibility. His personal distaste for some of Aristotle's beliefs, for example the Stagirite's anti-egalitarianism and approval of the mixed polity, was buttressed by a keen eye for critical weak points of the Aristotelian system. When he passes beyond generalized charges to specific criticisms of Aristotelian substantialism Hobbes often returns to the linguistic source of some of Aristotle's difficulties[25] and to the inadequacies of Aristotelian mechanics. Both in *De Corpore* and in the *Decameron Physiologicum*, Hobbes contends that the whole Aristotelian concept of substance originated in puzzles arising from the use of the copulative 'to be.' Citing that the concepts of substance and essence derive 'from the Latin verb *est*'[26] Hobbes argues that the elimination of that particular verb form would have eliminated the derivative concepts and the resulting difficulties. Historically, he points out in support of his argument, other languages without an analogous term managed to avoid the problem of essences.

> For having said in themselves (for example): 'a tree is a plant,' and conceiving well enough what is the signification of those names, knew not what to make of the word *is*, that couples those names; nor daring to call it a body, they called it by a new name (derived from the word *est*), *essentia* and *substantia*, deceived by the idiom of their own language. For in many other tongues, and namely in the

Hebrew, there is no such copulative. They thought the names of things sufficiently connected, when they are placed in their natural consequence; and were therefore never troubled with essences, nor other fallacy from the copulative 'est.'[27]

As a corollary to this line of argument, Hobbes asserts that many problems of Aristotelian modes of thought stem from the reification of accidents into abstract names, a process which the use of the copulative facilitates. Abstract names 'could have no being till there were propositions, from whose copula they proceed.'[28] Once these abstract names have been devised, he continues, men find that they can deal with them in thought as though they might be separated from all bodies. The confusion of separability in thought with separability in fact leads to 'the gross errors of writers of metaphysics,' allowing them to speak for example of 'insignificant words' such as abstract substance or separated essence.[29] Actually, Aristotle himself strove diligently to maintain that substances were not separate, only separable, from matter; herein lay the crux of his metaphysical dissent from Plato.[30] Aristotle did, however, believe that 'there are also incorporeal things,'[31] and this belief alone was enough to incur Hobbes's condemnation.

The real heart of Hobbes's assault upon the ontological status of abstract names was his radical nominalism. The Aristotelian tradition placed great significance in the definition of words, for the definition was the expression of the formulable essence of the thing described. The accurate, irreducible definition of a word was a revelation of the essential whatness of the substance represented by that word.[32] Consequently, definitions were beyond the whim of human will and served as the very basis of knowledge itself.[33] Furthermore, definitions served explanatory functions, for as Aristotle said, 'the "why" is reducible finally to the definition.'[34] Finally, the concept of definition expressed the order of creation or, to put it more accurately, 'imitative generation' within the Greek world view. 'Each substance,' Aristotle held, 'comes into being out of something that shares its name.'[35]

All these critically significant functions and attributes of definition are denied by Hobbes. Names, he says, do not express any immutable order in the world beyond the way in which we perceive it. The relationship of the name to the object is, in fact, dissolved by Hobbes, who considers names to be 'signs of our conceptions' and manifestly 'not signs of the things themselves.'[36] Since definitions are not expressions of any objective order, they are also no longer to be seen as independent of human will. Men, not the cosmos, are the source of words, and the invention of words may therefore be 'at pleasure.'

> A name is a word taken at pleasure to serve for a mark, which may raise in our mind a thought like to some thought we had before, . . . And it is for brevity's sake that I suppose the original of names to be arbitrary, judging it a thing that may be assumed as unquestionable. For considering that new names are daily made, and old ones laid aside; that diverse nations use different names, and how impossible it is either to observe similitude, or make any comparison betwixt a name and a thing, how can any man imagine that the names of things were imposed from their natures?[37]

Hobbes's strongest attack against the Aristotelian, realist notion of definition is levied against its function in explanation. As Basil Willey has observed in this context, the idea of explanation is itself not an immutable concept.[38] Something is termed a satisfactory explanation when it removes intellectual puzzlement, and there are various types of puzzlement. One of the chief features of the seventeenth-century's intellectual revolution, then, was a widespread shift in the type of puzzlement it felt and therefore in the nature of explanation which it accepted. To the seventeenth-century mind, the statement that something behaved in a particular way because that was its nature to do so may have constituted reassurance, but it certainly did not constitute an explanation. Such statements were for Hobbes and his contemporaries a part of a natural theodicy, perhaps, but they had no place in natural science. In an ultimate sense, of course, even modern natural science, when pushed by the question 'why?' can finally do no better than something like 'because that's just the way things are,' an expression logically though not psychologically parallel to the Aristotelian 'because that's according to nature.' The problem with the Scholastic version of Aristotle, however, was that this 'ultimate' kind of response came into play so early in the sequence of inquiry that it precluded the development of other legitimate, if more proximate, forms of explanation. It was largely this premature recourse to an ultimate mode of explanation that was responsible for the aridity of so much later Scholasticism, the paradigm of which was Moliere's doctoral candidate who was applauded for answering the question 'why does opium induce sleep?' with the response 'because of its dormative properties.'[39]

When the Galilean and Cartesian recourse to geometry as a method of inquiry led to the understanding of natural regularities which the Scholastic mode of inquiry had not even begun to clarify, the leading thinkers of the seventeenth-century's revolution were quick to substitute the new method for the older one. The general feeling was that the new light shed by geometry relieved them of the great, dull burden of the metaphysical subtleties that Hobbes derides as 'nothing else but Captions of Words.'[40] As Strauss has observed, Hobbes's praise of Plato is based upon his idea that Plato had 'freed himself from the spell of words.' 'Plato,' says Hobbes, 'that was the best philosopher of the Greeks, forbad entrance into his Schoole to all that were not in some measure geometricians.'[41] Unfortunately, however, the whole conception of teleology, purpose, and reason in the Aristotelian system was bound up with the critical role of definition, and the general glee with which the seventeenth-century thinkers unleashed themselves from the finite cosmos obscured but did not prevent the discard of these vital notions.

It was in the realm of physical mechanics that the new geometrical method was most fruitful and the older scheme more irredeemably barren by contrast. Therefore, Hobbes feels most secure in his nominalist attack when he couples his barbs against the explanatory function of Aristotelian definition with comments upon its sterility in the field of physics. When Aristotle attempted to explain the motion of bodies upward and downward, he appealed to their 'lightness' and 'heaviness' which he considered to be essences. 'But, be it noted, this is the question we are trying to answer—how can we account for the motion of light things and heavy things to their proper situation? The reason for it is that they have a natural tendency respectively towards a certain position: and this constitutes the essence of lightness and heaviness, the former being determined by an upward, the latter by a downward, tendency.'[42] By contrast with the mathematical regularities of falling bodies discovered by Galileo, this sort of account seemed poor fare indeed to Hobbes.

Then for Physiques, that is, the knowledge of the subordinate, and secundary causes of natural events; they render none at all, but empty words. If you desire to know why some kind of bodies sink naturally downwards toward the Earth, and others goe naturally from it; the School will tell you out of Aristotle, that the bodies that sink downward are Heavy; and that this Heavinesse is it that causes them to descend: But if you ask what they mean by Heavinesse, they will define it to be an endeavour to goe to the center of the Earth: so that the cause why things sink downward, is an endeavour to be below: which is as much as to say, that bodies descend, or ascend, because they doe.[43]

Having satisfied himself of the sterility of the Aristotelian realism and substantialism and perceiving the intimate connection between the two, Hobbes dismisses the Scholastic natural philosophy as 'rather a Dream than Science.'[44] The linguistic and ontological essentialism of Aristotelian thought had allowed natural causation to be accounted for by 'their own Ignorance, but disguised in other words.'[45] The elimination of substance from the universe removes the blockage to an understanding of natural causation, Hobbes feels, by rendering the universe susceptible of intelligibility through purely geometric and quantitative methods. In contrast to Aristotle, who saw matter as unintelligible in itself and substance therefore as an epistemological necessity, Hobbes sees the resolution of the world into 'body' as an epistemological breakthrough; for 'body' is 'Quantity,' the language of mathematics.[46]

Hobbes's conception of 'body,' the real 'stuff' of the universe, is basically a homogeneous, undifferentiated material substratum. The Aristotelian term *materia prima* is acceptable to Hobbes as a designation of 'body in general.' 'And what then is [*Materia Prima*]? A mere name; yet a name which is not of vain use; for it signifies a conception of body without the consideration of any form or other accident except only magnitude or extension, and aptness to receive form and other accident.'[47] The definition of 'body' then, is 'that, which having no dependence upon our thought is coincident or coextended with some part of space.'[48] Body is 'the thing placed,'[49] *res extensa*. It is 'objective,' existing independently of mind, 'real space' as contrasted with 'imaginary space' which is 'an effect on our imagination.'[50] It is equivalent to all real parts of the universe; and, considered as subject to accidents, it may be called substance.[51]

Now, strictly speaking, as Basil Willey has observed, the statement that 'all the universe is Body' has little or no positive meaning. Number, being abstract, has no real content, and 'body', as hypostasized number, is similarly empty.[52] The negative significance of the reduction of the universe to 'body' is far more potent, however; for the order and coherence of the universe had been expressed in the finite categories of substance. To reject the conception of substance, then, leads to an inescapable dissolution of the conception of universal order which it contained, unless some other expression of order is devised to provide a substitute. Clearly, 'body' does not provide this substitute. Any order that Hobbes leaves in his brave new world, then, comes through his idea of motion rather than through its correlate notion of body.

One clear example of this transposition of order and content from the substance/body aspect of the universe into motion is Hobbes's treatment of the notion of 'spirit.' In the language of the Schools, says Hobbes, spirits were conceived of as incorporeal substances. But since 'substance and body signifie the same thing'[53] the phrase 'incorporeal substance' constitutes a self-contradiction. The proper meaning of the word spirit, then, Hobbes concludes, is to refer to 'subtile bodies' which are nevertheless real and corporeal;[54] any other usage of the term must be 'metaphoricall', and these metaphorical uses of 'spirit' actually represent some form of motion or emotion. Thus the expression 'full of the Holy Spirit' may be understood as signifying zeal[55] or a 'working on their hearts,'[56] or simply 'life,'[57] which it must be recalled is merely a motion of limbs. Any time the word spirit is used, then, if it does not refer to an actual body, it must signify some kind of motion and not any impossible incorporeal substance.

In some ways this liberation of a human concept like 'spirit' from the substantialism of the Aristotelian tradition is a welcome achievement. The finitude and impenetrability of 'essence' and 'substance' language were not very cordial to philosophical accounts of personality, as the Church fathers had discovered at Nicea and Chalcedon. Hobbes is himself aware of these difficulties: 'And thus we have the exact meaning of the word "person," The Greek tongue cannot render it; for [the

Greek term signifies] properly a face, and metaphorically a vizard of an actor upon the stage. How then did the Greek Fathers render the word "person," as it is in the blessed Trinity? Not well. Instead of the word "person" they put "hypostasis," which signifies substance; from whence it might be inferred, that the three persons in the Trinity are three Divine substances, that is, three Gods.'[58] However, the virtue of the liberation which Hobbes effects is vitiated by the formlessness of the concept of motion which must bear the burden of providing the order and meaning that 'substance' gave, whatever defects that concept may have had. Consequently, the universe is liberated by Hobbes from the shackles of impenetrable substance only to be delivered into the anarchy of purely inertial motion.

NOTES

1. See Paul Shorey's statement, for example, that 'it will never be possible to clear up the confusion in Aristotle's *Metaphysics*, because Aristotle himself never cleared up that which existed in his own mind.' This and other comparable statements are cited by Joseph Owens, *The Doctrine of Being in the Aristotelian Metaphysics*, 2d ed. (Toronto: The Pontifical Institute of Medieval Studies, 1963), p. 107. Owens, himself, is inclined to defend Aristotle against most of these contentions, apparently feeling that Aristotle is 'consistently inconsistent' with a definite purpose.

2. Or, more strictly speaking, everything within the 'ordered' universe. For Aristotle there was still some 'chaos' around which was not a part of 'nature.' Hobbes makes no nature/chaos distinction.

3. Aristotle, *Metaphysics*, 6. 9. 1034a.

4. Ibid., 9. 1. 1045b.

5. See Owens, *The Doctrine of Being*, p. 139.

6. See for example *Metaphysics*, 7.

7. lbid.

8. Ibid., 7. 15. 1039b.

9. Ibid., 7. 16. 1041a.

10. Ibid., 12. 5. 1071a.

11. Ibid., 7. 17. 1041b.

12. Ibid., 7. 11. 1037a.

13. See Aristotle, *De Caelo*, 3 and 4.

14. See Aristotle, *De Anima*, 2.

15. Aristotle, *Metaphysics*, 9. 6. 1048b.

16. Suzanne Lilar in her study of eros in Western civilization speaks of 'the immense gulf between Plato's *eros* and Aristotle's *philia*.' Aristotle, she continues, took 'a kind of wicked pleasure in pinning love down to the dissection table.' 'Even the famous *catharsis* to which the name of Aristotle is wrongly linked (for the relevant passage in the *Poetica* is no more than a rather pale reference to that orgiastic purification which went back to the pre-Hellenic cults) has about it, as used by him, a feeling of the absence of any impulsiveness, ecstasy, or motive force' *Le Couple* (Paris: Bernard Grasset Press, 1963), pp. 55–59.

17. Aristotle, *Metaphysics*, 7. 3. 1029a.

18. Ibid., 7. 17. 1041a.

19. Ibid., 1. 8. 988b.

20. Ibid., 7. 10. 1036a.

21. See A. Schwegler's observation that: 'The term "substance" has taken on a meaning in modern philosophical terminology since Spinoza that is almost directly opposite to the sense of Aristotelian "ousia".' (Spragens' translation; quoted by Owens in German, *The Doctrine of Being*, p. 139).

22. John Locke, *Essay Concerning Human Understanding*, 2: 23, 2.

23. Hobbes, *Leviathan*, pp. 139–40.

24. Ibid., p. 589.

25. Some of Hobbes's remarks about the dangers of entanglement in linguistically induced snares seems rather prescient in light of modern linguistic analysis. Compare, for example, the following words of Hobbes to Wittgenstein's image of the

fly in the fly-bottle: 'From whence it happens, that they which trust to books, do as they cast up many little summes into a greater, without considering whether those little summes were rightly cast up or not; and at last finding the error visible, and not mistrusting their first grounds, know not which way to cleere themselves; but spend time in fluttering over their bookes; as birds that entring by the chimney, and finding themselves enclosed in a chamber, flutter at the false light of a glasse window, for want of wit to consider which way they came in' (*Leviathan*, p. 27).

26. Hobbes, *English Works*, 1: 34.

27. Ibid., 7: 81.

28. Ibid., 1: 33.

29. Ibid., p. 34.

30. E.g. 'Again, it would seem impossible that the substance and that of which it is the substance should exist apart; how, therefore, could the Ideas, being the substances of things, exist apart?' Aristotle, *Metaphysics*, 1. 9. 991b.

31. Aristotle, *Metaphysics*, 1. 8. 988b. See also the apparent belief of Aristotle that substances could exist apart even if they did not in fact do so: 'Some things can exist apart and some cannot, and it is the former that are substances' (*Metaphysics*, 12. 5. 1071a).

32. See Aristotle, *Metaphysics*, 1 and 2.

33. For example: 'Further, those who speak thus (i.e. to the effect that essences are reducible) destroy science; for it is not possible to have this till one comes to the unanalyzable terms' (*Metaphysics* 2. 2. 994b).

34. Aristotle, *Metaphysics*, 1. 3. 983a.

35. *Ibid.*, 12. 3. 1070a. It was this idea, of course, which lay behind the Greek inability to conceive of evolution in the way that we now understand it.

36. Hobbes, *English Works*, 1: 17.

37. Ibid., 1 : 16.

38. See Basil Willey, *The Seventeenth Century Background* (New York: Doubleday Anchor Books, 1953), Chapt. 1.

39. Candidate: Mihi a docto doctore
                Domandatur causam et rationem quare
                Opium facit dormire,
                A quoi respondeo:
                Quia est in eo
                Vertus dormitiva,
                Cuius est natura
                Sensus assoupire.

Chorus of examiners: Bene bene bene respondere.
                     Dignus, dignus est intrare
                     In nostro docto corpore.

Quoted by R. G. Collingwood, *The Idea of Nature* (New York: Oxford University Press, 1960), p. 93.

40. Hobbes, *Leviathan*, p. 589.

41. Ibid., p. 588.

42. Aristotle *Physics* 8. 4. 255b.

43. Hobbes, *Leviathan*, p. 597.

44. Ibid., p. 588.

45. Ibid., p. 598.

46. 'Quantity is nothing else but the Determination of Matter; that is to say of Body' (Ibid.).

47. Hobbes, *English Works*, 1: 118.

48. Ibid., p. 102.

49. Ibid., p. 105.

50. Ibid.

51. Hobbes, *Leviathan*, pp. 339–40.

52. See *Seventeenth Century Background*, pp. 100–101, 104.

53. Hobbes, *Leviathan*, p. 340.

54. 'But when he hath so formed them (i.e. spirits) they are Substances, endued with dimensions, and take up roome, and can be moved from place to place, which is peculiar to Bodies: and therefore are not Ghosts incorporeall, that is to say Ghosts that are in *no place*; that is to say that are *no where*; that is to say, that seeming to be somewhat, are *nothing*' (*Leviathan*, p. 345). Notice in the parallelism of the final three clauses Hobbes's equation of spatiality and reality.

55. Hobbes, *Leviathan*, p. 344.
56. Ibid., p. 352.
57. Ibid., p. 343.
58. Hobbes, *English Works*, 4: 311.

4

The Disordering of Nature

'Nature is everywhere the cause of order.' — *Aristotle*

'Nature dissociates, and renders men apt to invade and destroy one another.' — *Hobbes*

The critical transformations which Hobbes performs upon the root concepts of motion and substance lead quite logically to an equally new, radically transformed concept of nature. In the Aristotelian system, substance and movement were the two components which together comprised the realm of nature, so the sharp change in the way the parts were envisaged implied a corresponding change in the complex whole which they were seen to form. In short, once again Hobbes follows the formal pattern of the basic Aristotelian world-framework, after having effected his key substantive changes.

The linkage between the concept of motion and the image of nature is quite clear and direct in both Aristotle and Hobbes. Hobbes's utter infatuation with the Galilean view of motion rests upon his conviction that it provides the key to understanding the entire natural world. This conviction Hobbes makes manifest in his dedicatory epistle to *De Corpore*. The direct link between nature and motion is the reason Galileo is viewed as having opened the 'gate of natural philosophy universal.'

Formally and methodologically, Hobbes is simply following Aristotle's path. The very definition of 'natural' for Aristotle turned around the possession of the capacity for movement. 'All the things mentioned present a feature in which they differ

G

from things which are *not* constituted by nature. Each of them has *within itself* a principle of motion and of stationariness (in respect to place, or of growth and decrease, or by way of alteration) . . . which seems to indicate that nature is a source or cause of being moved and of being at rest in that to which it belongs primarily.'[1] Since nature 'is a source or cause of being moved,' inquiry into nature logically must begin with an inquiry into motion, for the structure of movement determines the structure of nature. 'Nature has been defined as "a principle of motion and change," and it is the subject of our inquiry. We must therefore see that we understand the principle of "motion," for if it were unknown, the meaning of "nature" too would be unknown.'[2]

The Aristotelian analysis of movement which followed upon this methodological program led to the model of movement as 'the fulfillment of what exists potentially, in so far as it exists potentially.'[3] On the basis of this analysis, then, nature was depicted as a hierarchical series of finite substances, each moving in an orderly fashion toward its *telos*. Nonteleological movements were not considered by Aristotle to belong to nature at all; they belonged to the category of pure chance, or 'spontaneity.'[4] Nature itself, Aristotle insisted, 'belongs to the class of causes which act for the sake of something.'[5]

In Aristotle, the concept of nature in combination with the idea of the 'unmoved movers' assumed the role of organizing principle in the universe which had been given by Plato largely to the soul.[6] All living things, and even the inanimate simple bodies, became endowed by Aristotle with the inherent tendency to movements of a particular sort, and teleology, 'working for the sake of a cause,' was made a feature of the entire natural order. The whole natural universe was made 'rational,' modeled on the paradigm of purposeful action. 'When one man said, then,' contended Aristotle, 'that reason was present—as in animals, so throughout nature—as the cause of order and all arrangement, he seemed like a sober man in contrast with the random talk of his predecessors.'[7]

Throughout the whole Aristotelian discussion of nature, then, ran the omnipresent theme of order. In the eighth book of the *Physics*, Aristotle summarized the coherence and orderliness which he saw as definitive of nature, saying 'that which is produced or directed by nature can never be anything disorderly: for nature is everywhere the cause of order.'[8] Things formed by nature, like those formed by human *techne*, were envisioned as formed 'for the sake of an end.'[9] To continue this analogy between the working of nature and the working of human craft, Aristotle spoke of 'mistakes' in nature, as when monstrosities are produced, as reflecting a 'failure in the purposive effort.'[10]

The view of nature as a coherent whole which everywhere worked for order exerted a profound influence on the political ideas of the Aristotelian and Scholastic traditions. The broad scope of nature, after all, encompassed that rational animal, man, and his social life as much as it encompassed the movements of plants, insects, and animals. The human community, or polis, was itself seen as a product of nature, a fruition of some of the natural tendencies or strivings inherent in the human psyche. The organization of the polis constituted a natural *telos*. 'Because it is the completion of associations existing by nature, every polis exists by nature, having itself the same quality as the earlier associations from which it grew. It is the end or consummation to which those associations move, and the nature of things exists in their end or consummation; for what each thing is when its growth is completed we call the nature of that thing, whether it be a man or a horse or a family.'[11]

Man is, therefore, 'by nature an animal intended to live in a polis.'[12] Anyone who does not live in a political order is either a beast or some sort of god, for the immanent strivings of human nature depend upon a political setting for their fulfillment. Some of man's peculiar faculties, such as his capacity to perceive good and evil and his linguistic abilities, are intrinsically social faculties. Only through political intercourse are they put to use; and since nature makes nothing in vain, nature obviously intends man to be a political animal. A man without a polis is without the necessary environment to be what he is by nature. He is 'in the position of a solitary advanced piece in a game of draughts.'[13]

The polis was prior to the individual, for in Aristotelian nature 'the whole is necessarily prior to the part.'[14] For this reason, and because man is dependent on the existence of the polis for the fulfillment of his own nature, it follows that nature itself is a source of political obligation. That is, a man is bound to behave such and such a way with respect to his fellows and with respect to the polis because that is his nature. He must respect the necessities of political organization and behave accordingly, or he thwarts the requirements of his own fulfillment. It becomes possible, therefore, to speak of natural laws which have political content. The commands of natural law were the logical consequences for action derived from the teleological order of nature, and they made sense only because of the tension between the potential and the actual which was seen as characteristic of nature as a whole. Violations of the natural law were 'mistakes' in the sense that Aristotle used that term, acts which led to a corruption of the 'natural' development of the human and political world toward its *telos*. It will be necessary to return to this problem shortly, but for the moment the essential point is the dependence of the natural law notion upon the holistic and teleological conception of nature which produced it.

Visualizing man and politics as a part of 'nature' so conceived generated some conceptual difficulties. Some of these problems grew from the overextension of the teleological model to apply it to the phenomena of physical motion. The broad scope of the model gave it its breadth and nobility. But by extending the model of purposeful movement beyond its genuinely applicable range, Aristotle gave his whole concept of nature an Achilles heel which led to its virtual destruction in the seventeenth century.

The other principal locale of conceptual difficulties attendant upon the application of the model of 'natural movement' to the full range of reality came at the human end of the hierarchy. These problems appeared most sharply in the attempt to embody certain theological ideas in Greek philosophical terminology. The incredible battles fought in the early Church councils over the relationship of person and substance were but one expression of the inadequacies of substantialism in dealing with human affairs. Other examples were the difficulties of conceiving the Christian God in terms of the Aristotelian unmoved mover, difficulties reflected in Pascal's observation of the difference between the God of Abraham and the deity of the philosophers, and the problems encountered in characterizing time and history.

Hobbes was aware of both of these key areas of anomaly in the use of the Aristotelian concept of nature. Time and again he heaps scorn upon the Scholastic teleological accounts of physical motions. And, especially in his debates with Bishop Bramhall, Hobbes demonstrates a keen grasp of some of the theological difficulties produced by the uncritical use of Aristotelian concepts. However, and this step is critical, Hobbes feels that he can solve these problems within the Aristotelian format—i.e., within the model of a single, all-encompassing realm of 'nature'—once he has transformed the substantive image of what nature is. In other words, rather than rejecting the entire Aristotelian model of reality, he assumes that its framework is acceptable if its substance is changed in accordance with the inertial model of motion.

The persistence of this Aristotelian cosmological matrix which designates human and political forms as one species of natural form provides Hobbes with the setting of his systematic political speculations. Like the exponents of the Aristotelian tradition, Hobbes derives significant political implications from the character of the 'natural' world of which politics is one part. These implications are important and, by contrast with the tradition against which Hobbes is reacting, quite novel.

Because Hobbes views motion as something very different from the Aristotelian actualization of potential, he sees nature as something very different from the Aristotelian ordered whole; therefore his theories must logically presume a radically altered environment for political phenomena. The new face of nature is not that of something which possesses an inherent tendency toward growth and fulfillment, but rather of something which merely persists in its motion without end. The new world of nature is not a cause of order but rather the absence of order. The whole is not prior to the parts, but the parts are the realities and the wholes merely works of artifice. The impact of this deep transformation of politics' setting, nature, is manifest in Hobbes's political analyses.

The novelty of the Hobbesian understanding of nature and its political import are first evidenced in his construct of the state of nature. The natural condition of man, as depicted by Hobbes, provides a stark contrast to the Aristotelian picture of man as a political animal by nature. The Greek belief that man is a creature 'born fit for society' is, Hobbes says, 'certainly false, and an error proceeding from our too slight contemplation of human nature.'[15] Men do desire to come together; but merely coming together does not constitute a society, for 'civil societies are not mere meetings, but bonds.'[16] Men seek the company and services of other men, but for their own advantage. Specifically, men seek congress with their fellows 'either for gain or for glory'; and these could actually be better attained by dominion than by belonging to society as one member among others. 'But though the benefits of this life may be much furthered by mutual help; since yet those may be better attained to by dominion than by the society of others, I hope no body will doubt, but that men would much more greedily be carried by nature, if all fear were removed, to obtain dominion, than to gain society.'[17]

Man's natural condition, then, far from being that of an organized society, is a state of mutual enmity. In fact, 'without a common Power to keep them all in awe, they are in that condition which is called Warre; and such a warre, as is of every man, against every man.'[18] In a famous passage, Hobbes itemizes some of the ways in which this natural situation is truly an 'ill condition': 'In such condition, there is no place for Industry; because the fruit thereof is uncertain: and consequently no Culture of the Earth, no Navigation, nor use of the commodities that may be imported by sea; no commodious Building; no Instruments of moving, and removing such things as require much force; no Knowledge of the face of the Earth; no amount of Time; no Arts; no letters; no Society; and what is worst of all, continuall feare, and danger of violent death; And the life of man, solitary, poore, nasty, brutish, and short.'[19]

The causes of such a sorry state may be found in the relative equality of human endowments and the nature of human desires. Men differ to a certain extent in their natural aptitudes and abilities, of course; but on the whole, says Hobbes, they are sufficiently equal both in physical and mental faculties that no 'one man can thereupon claim to himself any benefit, to which another may not pretend, as well as he.'[20] From this rough equality of ability arises a basic equality of 'hope in the attaining of our ends.' This pattern quickly leads to conflict, however, since 'many men at the same time have an appetite to the same thing; which yet very often they can neither enjoy it in common nor yet divide it.'[21] Especially is this inability for all to be satisfied in their aims manifest in the quest for glory, which Hobbes feels to be a very important human motivation. For vainglory can be satisfied only by a relative pre-eminence; 'if all men have it no man hath it, for they consist in comparison and precellence.'[22] Therefore, one man's attainment of his goal is intrinsically dependent upon the thwarting of his fellows' similar desires.

This stark analysis of the human condition which Hobbes presents grows from several sources. In part, it simply reflects a very different substantive assessment of human desires and motivation from that of the Aristotelian tradition. Hobbes sees a rather large degree of ruthless egocentricity as a general human trait, and he is therefore not predisposed to see the construction of a viable civil society as a painless feat. The political turbulence and consequent social disorder during his own lifetime lent credence to his vision. For example, Hobbes suggests that the upheavals of civil war, which he experienced, offer a good approximation of the state of nature.[23]

While this substantively bleak view of the human psyche is a departure from the Aristotelian outlook, it is not wholly novel. Hobbes shares much in common with the Augustinian tradition, for example, with its sober assessment of political possibilities based on its analysis of the profound and pervasive sinfulness of the human spirit. The vainglory of Hobbesian man resembles the *amor sui* of the Augustinian sinner. And the warlike societies of Hobbes bear a noteworthy semblance to Augustine's 'robber bands.' The analogies should not be overdrawn, for the Hobbesian system is without the Platonic philosophical and theological context of the Augustinian world view, and this difference is significant. Nevertheless, the resemblances are real, and they serve to remind us that Hobbes's divergence from Aristotle in his account of human nature is not substantively without precedent.

This source of Hobbes's departure from the Aristotelian tradition, that is, his basically different account of human nature is an important one. Hobbes's account of the state of nature is more than this, however. It also possesses a methodological and substantive significance which develops out of the new natural philosophy which Hobbes affirms. This significance needs to be recognized if it is to be appreciated that Hobbes's political concepts are to some extent a function of his new cosmological paradigm and are not purely the outcome of his observations of men and manners.

In Aristotle and in Aquinas the idea of nature as a teleological system of order undergirded their statements about human nature. Since nature was composed of substances directed toward their completion, statements about the 'nature' of anything, including man, had to take into account not only origins, but the end as well. The process of assigning a 'nature' to something was a matter of defining its essential 'whatness,' and the goal toward which it moved was actually the determinative influence in this definition. This intellectual method was in accord with the ontology which sustained it, and both the method and the ontology could be seen in Aristotle's contention that 'it is the goal rather than the starting point of motion that gives its name to a particular process of change.'[24] The depiction of the 'nature' of something, then, inevitably involved the consideration of the entire pattern of its movement, not only including but emphasizing its *telos* or perfection. When Aristotle said that man is by nature a social animal, then, he did not necessarily mean that man was instinctively or by origin a social creature, but rather that his faculties were such that they could be fully realized only in society.

If, methodologically, the Aristotelian tradition looked to the end of something to ascertain its nature, Hobbes in contrast looks to its simplest component elements. This change constitutes a striking methodological reversal, pregnant with substantive implications. In making this change, Hobbes was participating in one of the key facets of the seventeenth-century revolution, namely, the espousal of a new method whose principal exponent was Descartes. 'The whole of human knowledge,' according to Descartes, 'consists in a distinct perception of the way in which simple natures combine in order to build up other objects.'[25] The right method of discovering the first principles of something, then, is on this view to separate it into its components. This process is termed 'resolution' by Hobbes, and at times he even equates it with reason.[26] In any case, it is resolution which brings us to 'universal knowledge.' 'And in this manner, by resolving continually, we may come to know what those things are, whose causes being first known severally, and afterwards compounded, bring us to the knowledge of singular things. I conclude, therefore, that the method of attaining to the

universal knowledge of things, is purely analytical.'[27] Once
this process of resolution is completed, Hobbes feels, further
inquiry can be conducted simply by using the principles of
motion, for all things have 'but one universal cause, which is
motion.'

Hobbes's state of nature, then, is a theoretical construct
produced through an analytical procedure of this kind.
It is a picture of civil society as Hobbes sees it, with all the
civil bonds dissolved by a process of abstraction. The human
animal which inhabits Hobbes's mythical state of nature is
not the Aristotelian animal who exists in tension between
his origin and his fulfillment, nor is he simply 'instinctive'
man antecedent to all society (a creature that would be pure
fiction); but he is rather the typical seventeenth-century
man as Hobbes sees him, released from the network of institutions and obligations which constitute society. C. B.
MacPherson, who emphasizes the connection of Hobbes to a
possessive market society, has recognized this function of
Hobbes's state of nature quite clearly, characterizing it as
'the hypothetical condition in which men as they now are,
with natures formed by living in civilized society, would
necessarily find themselves if there were no common power
able to overawe them all.'[28] MacPherson's attempt to attribute
Hobbes's psychology to a peculiar social origin is perhaps
overdrawn; the quest for gain and glory which Hobbes so
vividly depicts is not confined to capitalism, but seems to find
expression in traditional and modern totalitarian societies as
well. However, his perception of Hobbes's state of nature as
'reached by successive degrees of abstraction from civilized
society'[29] is not dependent upon his sociological explanation
of its content.

The method for discovering what is 'natural' about anything,
including men and political society, then, is for Hobbes this
process of analytical dissolution which he calls 'resolution.'
As Rousseau acutely was to observe in the next century, he
actually failed to complete his appointed analytical task. What

he depicted as man in the state of nature was still a political animal, one who was released from the bonds of obligation and authority but who was still clearly a social product.[30] Nevertheless, whatever failings Hobbes had in carrying out his analysis, the nature of the intellectual project he had in mind is quite clear: to reach the 'real' components of any 'complex whole' such as political society, one must intellectually 'resolve' it into its constituent elements.

This norm for intellectual analysis, it is important to recognize, does not arise from a vacuum. Instead, it is the methodological imperative which follows from the new view of nature which Hobbes shared with his distinguished contemporaries. The new method, the new epistemology, which produces the new motif of the 'state of nature' rests firmly on an ontological foundation. The analyst must resolve to find what is real not because of some intellectual whim, but because nature is itself a state of dissolution and dissociation. In the context of political analysis, Hobbes denies the ontological priority, the natural order, of society, not simply because man is seen as power-hungry, but because the ontological priority of all complex wholes disappears in the seventeenth century.

The new understanding of nature as a state where order is lacking is most strikingly captured in Hobbes's references to 'meer nature.'[31] This characterization would have been nonsensical to Aristotle and the Scholastics. For them, after all, nature was everywhere the cause of order, the fundamental force in the world acting for coherence and organization. But Hobbes's 'meer nature' is no organic purposeful whole; it is an atomistic agglomeration of entities not related by nature. A corollary of the 'simplicity' of nature which seemed so admirable and intelligible to the seventeenth-century mind was its disorganization. In a certain sense, the new nature is exquisitely ordered—but the criteria of this order are purely and exhaustively geometric; any other form of order, such as political or moral order, is artificial.

Hobbes goes even further. Nature is not only characterized

by a lack of human or political order; it is even a force working against order in some ways. 'Nature dissociates,' he says, 'and renders men apt to invade and destroy one another.'[32] The 'natural lusts of men,' he says elsewhere, 'do daily threaten each other.'[33] The political task which faces men, therefore, is not to attain that order which nature has provided for them, but rather to escape the intrinsically ill condition of meer nature.

The disorder of meer nature, standing as it does in such stark contrast to the orderliness of Aristotelian nature, helps to explain the radically creative force which Hobbes attributes to the word of the sovereign. Given the anarchy of meer nature, the voice of the sovereign must serve as the *logos*— the origin of order. For nature herself is now bereft of its *logos*; it has been stripped altogether of its ordering force. Man must therefore create and invest such a force on his own as a work of artifice. He must build 'an Artificiall Man . . . of greater stature and strength than the Naturall for whose protection and defense it was intended,' namely, 'that great Leviathan.'[34] Only through such a creation can man save himself from the suicidal consequences of remaining in a state of nature.

The dissolution of the teleological orderliness of nature carries with it some further important consequences for Hobbes's social thought, as well. In the first place, all moral judgments are deprived of any objective foundation and therefore must be seen as purely expressions of subjective appetite. In parallel fashion, any standards external to the vagaries of human will disappear from consideration of economics. And finally, the meaning and content of 'natural law' undergoes a striking substantive deflation. Each of these developments will be considered in its turn.

In the classical tradition, ethics was a branch of ontology. Moral judgments were extrapolations from the 'nature of things' for human action. The logical form of an ethical imperative was something like this: 'If the order of the universe is such-and-such, then one should act in such-and-such a way for his actions to be consonant with that order.' Specific injunctions to behave in a particular way were, then, basically hypothetical imperatives, based upon the reality principle. That is, man did not create the order of the world, and he cannot abolish it. Therefore, he must reconcile his own actions to the givens of the order within which he lives. The alternative is to be irrational in a very profound sense, or insane.

This understanding of ethical discourse is obviously contingent upon certain prior ontological assumptions for its validity. Specifically, unless one presumes some form of teleological order in the world, the reality principle loses any real force as the source of imperatives for action. Only an ordered nature of this kind can provide ethical statements or moral judgments with any real substance. The ethical tension between 'ought' and 'is' is grounded in the ontological tension between essence and existence; and if the latter is dissolved, then the former falls apart as well. Precisely this kind of ontological transformation occurs in Hobbes's cosmology, so appropriately enough the whole nature and status of ethical discourse is altered as well, as Hobbes himself clearly recognizes and forthrightly affirms.

With the disappearance of a logos from nature, the only order left is that of natural lust. That is, the mandates of natural reason are deprived of any ontological basis and their role must henceforth be performed by the only compelling natural quality left, namely, the will, which is the aggregate of the natural motions, appetite and aversion. Ethical statements, therefore, must be expressions of will, or to use the more contemporary term, expressions of preference. There is nothing else in nature for them to express. Hobbes's theory of ethical propositions, then, is a perfect prototype for what has more recently become known as the emotive theory of ethics. 'But whatsoever is the object of any man's appetite or desire; that is it, which he for his part calleth good; and the object of his hate, and aversion, Evill; and of his contempt, Vile and

Inconsiderable. For these words of Good, Evill, and Contemptible, are ever used with relation to the person that useth them: There being nothing simply and absolutely so; nor any common Rule of Good and Evill, to be taken from the nature of the objects themselves.'[35]

The ramifications of this position extends into Hobbes's doctrines in the area of political economy and economic justice. Viewing economic activity as only one aspect of a broader human order, the Aristotelian tradition placed certain limitations upon it which followed from the larger order. The demands of economic justice were expressions of the belief that commerce must be integrated into a wider framework of human nature, and these demands had been elaborated in theories of just price, commutative justice, and distributive justice. Here, as elsewhere, however, the concept of justice is an ontological one, and Hobbes's destruction of the classical ontology leaves him no basis for these traditional theories of economic justice. Hobbes therefore concludes, again quite logically from his premises, that the only criterion of value is 'appetite,' and hence there is no distinction between value and market price. Just (from 'justice') price gives way to just (merely) price. 'Justice of Actions, is by writers divided into commutative, Distributive; . . . Commutative they place in the equality of value of the things contracted for; and distributive, in the distribution of equall benefit, to men of equall merit. As if it were Injustice to sell dearer than we buy; or to give more to a man than he merits. The value of all things contracted for, is measured by the Appetite of the Contractors: and therefore the just value, is that which they be contented to give.'[36]

Just compensation for the use of other human beings, Hobbes continues, as in the case of raw materials and finished goods, is properly to be determined by the will of the employer. 'The value, or Worth of a man, is as of all other things, his Price; that is to say, so much as would be given for the use of his Power: and therefore is not absolute; but a thing dependent on the need and judgment of another.'[37] Considered as simply an empirical theory about the mechanisms of price determination in a market economy, of course, this account is unexceptionable. Considered as a theory of economic justice, however, Hobbes's pronouncements represent a complete relinquishing of moral control over the market. Rather than being a contingent facet of human social life, economic relations become the autonomous standard to which all other facets of political order must conform.

This theory provided a very useful tenet for emergent capitalism. The laissez faire economists of classical liberalism were soon to turn the unfettered operation of the market mechanism into an immutable law of nature, ostensibly beyond the scope of human control. This notion presumably salved the consciences of the new entrepreneurial class; however, capitalism's tendency to carry the Hobbesian theory of a man's value to its logical conclusion eventually elicited anguished responses. Marxian economics, for example, which begins with a labor theory of value and thence derives concepts such as 'exploitation' and 'alienation,' is actually a systematic restitution of economics to a contingent place within the entire human economy and has a root affinity with the classical concepts of just price and distributive justice. Contemporary economists who think that Marx's use of the labor theory of value was simply a bad misconception of the functioning of a market system miss the point entirely; for the Marxian system was normative in the classical sense, that is, anchored in a humanized ontology. A market economy wholly unchastened by such anthropocentric concepts must ultimately prove intolerable; and Western capitalism has, in fact, averted a Marxian cataclysm only by implicitly repudiating the unfettered Hobbesian theory through new channels of distributive justice such as the progressive income tax.

A final political ramification of the radical alteration in the understanding of 'nature' effected by Hobbes appears in his consideration of the laws of nature. The question of the meaning, status, and content of natural laws is a critical one in the interpretation of Hobbes. The importance of this question arises both historically and logically. Historically, it is an important issue because of the central position which natural law held in the political theory of the Aristotelian-Scholastic tradition against which Hobbes reacted. Logically, the question of natural law is also important because of its intimate connection with the whole problem of the grounds of political obligation; and the designation of the source and extent of political obligation is a central issue, if not *the* central issue, in any systematic political theory.

Unfortunately, as is often the case, this absolutely central question is also an extremely vexing one which has, accordingly, given rise to several divergent theories about Hobbes's real meaning and intent. There are two principal reasons for the peculiar difficulties which surround the whole problem of Hobbes's views on natural law. First, there are some very deep semantic problems which systematically complicate the entire question. Second, Hobbes's statements about natural law often do not appear wholly reconcilable with each other for varied reasons.

The semantic problems involved, in turn, derive from at least two sources: first, the inherent multiplicity of linguistic functions performed by the key terms, and, second, the substantive transformation effected in some of these terms by implication from the basic paradigm transformation we have been examining. Both of these sources of semantic difficulty can be appreciated by considering the three central terms themselves, namely 'natural,' 'law,' and 'obligation.'

The term natural is used in a variety of ways in common discourse. In a general sense, we often refer to the 'nature' of something, meaning its irreducible defining properties, attributes, and functions. This usage is a kind of colloquial remnant of the more systematic identification of nature with essence in the Aristotelian tradition. 'Nature' also may be used to designate a particular class of things, which may be distinguished from other classes such as supernatural, human, historical, or artificial. And finally, 'natural' may refer to a specific mode of action, as when we say that such-and-such happened quite 'naturally.' This family of meanings only begins the semantic tangle, however, for ambiguity may attend each of these general significations. For example, to say that something naturally occurred may refer to economic rationality, psychological compulsion, or biological and physical invariance.[38]

These semantic problems are compounded by the various substantive interpretations which each of the usages may represent, depending upon the implicit cosmology involved. As R. G. Collingwood has lucidly demonstrated, the substantive reference of nature in terms of both what is included within it and what is seen as its characteristic mode of action has varied significantly within the Western philosophical tradition.[39] These transformations in what, substantively, is perceived as natural, of course, can cause great confusion in assessing the meaning of the term in another era. For example, what appears as a logical *faux pas*, the 'naturalistic fallacy,' may not be that, given a different understanding of nature. It is important, therefore, in approaching a topic such as Hobbes's views on natural law, not to begin by facilely setting up logical categories which are dependent upon our own substantive philosophical premises.

'Law' can also suffer from ambiguity. For example, we may use the term law to refer to such varied phenomena as statistical regularity (Boyle's law), natural compulsion (the law of gravity), political promulgations (the Taft-Hartley law), and moral dictates (the law of the prophets). It is partly for this reason that Hobbes tries to specify a narrow signification of the term to refer solely to the 'command of him or them that have coercive power.'[40] This semantic recommendation, however, as is often the case in such questions, has both ontological roots and political ramifications. Ontologically, this limitation of law to a species of command reflects Hobbes's radical nominalism.

For Aristotle, for the Stoics, for Scholastic theorists such as Aquinas or Hooker, law was a manifestation of the universal *logos*, a product of the reason which pervaded the created order. Positive laws, products of the human will, were recognized by this tradition, but they were always viewed in the context of the natural and divine laws which transcended human volition. For Hobbes, however, nature is governed by no rational, purposeful *logos* of this sort. Given this premise, it makes very good sense to clarify the concept of law by confining it to the realm of will, of command, and removing the ambiguity that occurred when the component of rationality was insisted upon as a defining feature. Furthermore, this semantic clarification has the added implication that only the sovereign can say what is lawful; for many can claim to be rational, but only the sovereign possesses coercive power of an overriding degree. Hobbes was hardly unaware of or displeased by this implication of his definition of law.

Finally, the semantic problems attending the intimately related concept of obligation are at least as thick as those surrounding nature and law. Therefore the attempt to ascertain whether the laws of nature are obligatory in Hobbes is complicated by a geometric progression of definitional difficulties. To be obliged in its most general sense means to be bound, and Hobbes asserts his faithfulness to this basic meaning. But there are many kinds of bondage, and hence many kinds of obligation as well. Michael Oakeshott distinguishes four kinds of obligation, for example, which he calls physical, rational, moral and political.[41] Thus, one may be 'obliged' to slow down when driving his Volkswagen up a steep hill, he may be 'obliged' to give assent to a proposition of Euclidean geometry, he may be 'obliged' to care for his ageing parents, and he may be 'obliged' to pay his taxes.

The meaning of obligation is further complicated, as in the case of 'nature' and 'law,' by substantive philosophical considerations. These considerations lead to some varied conceptions of what must be involved in a genuine theory of obligation. It is generally understood that a theory of political obligation should derive political obligation from some source outside of politics narrowly defined; otherwise, the question of legitimacy is begged and the question of obligation becomes a redundancy for the purely empirical problem of 'who governs?' However, what these possible outside sources are from which political obligation may be properly derived may vary with philosophical persuasion. For example, since Hume it has generally been held that no 'ought' can legitimately be derived from an 'is.' This ground rule places certain clear limitations upon a theory of political obligation. However, this limitation derives its force from an ontology which denies the presence of tension between potentiality and actuality within the realm of 'is.' It was for this reason that Hume's 'logical' rule was not 'discovered' until his time.

Besides these deep and pervasive semantic problems, the status of laws of nature in Hobbes's system is complicated by at least two idiosyncrasies of Hobbes's thought on this question. In the first place, Hobbes at times simply seems to be inconsistent, sometimes attributing features to the natural law quite offhandedly which are never reconciled with other accounts which would seem to exclude them. For example, at one point Hobbes implies a very broad and inclusive scope to laws of nature in a simple appositive phrase: 'The first are the same Lawes of Nature, of which I have spoken already in the 14th and 15th chapters of this Treatise; namely, Equity, Justice, Mercy, Humility, and the rest of the Morall Vertues.'[42] Referring back to chapters fourteen and fifteen, however, the reader will be hard pressed indeed to find anything resembling this catalog of virtues allegedly encompassed by the laws of nature; and the rationale of their inclusion in the laws of nature as Hobbes systematically defines them elsewhere remains highly problematic. Second, as I will argue shortly, Hobbes is willing to attribute a dual status to the laws of nature, which in turn implies the possibility of deriving political obligation from more than one source. There is nothing illicit in giving a dual status to the laws of nature, of course; but this feature, together with Hobbes's occasional vagueness and inconsistency, adds one more complication to the overall picture.

With these warnings as to the numerous potential pitfalls surrounding this problem, we can turn to consider the laws of nature in Hobbes, their meaning, their significance, and in what way or ways they are obliging. Considerable clarity, I hope, can be given to this question by understanding Hobbes's laws of nature as one more embodiment of the basic pattern of paradigm transformation which we have perceived throughout his system of ideas. That is, once again Hobbes's concepts retain the framework of the Aristotelian and Scholastic formulation but reach a different set of conclusions because of the transformation of key substantive models.

There are essentially two standard accounts of the nature and status of Hobbes's laws of nature. The first interpretation sees them as prudential maxims which will recommend themselves by their logical force to any man desirous of avoiding violent death. The second interpretation, generally associated with A. E. Taylor and Howard Warrender, takes a different tack. According to this argument, the first interpretation is unsatisfactory because laws of nature so conceived would not be genuinely obligatory. If they are not genuinely obligatory, moreover, the argument runs, then Hobbes cannot claim to have established any binding duty to obey the civil law, for a duty to obey the civil law 'cannot be prescribed by civil law itself.'[43] Hobbes clearly feels that he has established the obligation to obey civil authority, though, and he therefore must feel the laws of nature, from which the civil authority is derived, to be obligatory also. This conclusion is buttressed, moreover, by the fact that he continues to speak of natural laws after he has clearly defined laws as commands and equally clearly distinguished command from counsel.[44] If the laws of nature are but prudential maxims, the argument goes, they could not be genuinely obligatory, for a man 'cannot be obliged to do as he is Counselled, because the hurt of not following it, is his own.'[45] These difficulties disappear, however, if the laws of nature are regarded not as prudential maxims but as commands of one who has the right to do so, namely, God. As Taylor concludes, then, 'I can only make Hobbes's statements consistent with each other by supposing that he meant quite seriously what he so often says, that the "natural law" is the command of God, and to be obeyed *because* it is God's command.'[46]

Actually, both of these interpretations are correct, at least in what they affirm about Hobbes's laws of nature, even if they are not correct in what they deny. Hobbes provides two lines of argument for the grounding of political obligation, both of which he is perfectly willing to affirm, and each of which is quite compatible with the other. The laws of nature play a central role in both lines of argument; and in fact their content is identical in each case, although their status differs. Hobbes is himself indifferent as to which argument is accepted, for either way he has reached the same conclusions.

The dual status which Hobbes accords to the laws of nature is clearly reflected in the passage where he says of them: 'These dictates of Reason, men use to call by the name of Lawes; but improperly: for they are but Conclusions, or Theoremes concerning what conduceth to the conservation and defense of themselves; whereas Law, properly is the word of him, that by right hath command over others. But yet if we consider the same Theorems, as delivered, in the word of God, that by right commandeth all things; then they are properly called Lawes.'[47] Having said this, Hobbes can quite legitimately refer to natural laws as both counsels and commands. They are both dictates of prudence derived from an understanding of the nature of things and dictates of God, who is the author of nature. Viewing them in the guise of divine commands neither adds nor subtracts anything in the way of substance from the laws of nature; it simply accords to them a status of moral obligatoriness which they do not possess merely as counsels of prudence.

There is nothing especially novel about this attribution of a double status to laws of nature, actually. It was a commonplace of the Christian natural law theorists, whether the Catholic Thomas or the Anglican Hooker, that the laws of nature could be grounded autonomously in the structure of the created order or grounded in the will of God who had created that order. The epistemological situation was seen, moreover, as paralleling the ontological pattern of dual status. One could know the laws of nature by the exercise of his natural reason, but they could also be found in the scriptural and prophetic revelation of God's imperatives. Hobbes's theoretical radicalism in relation to natural laws consists not in the status he accords them but in the substance he ascribes to them.

Some commentators, Warrender and Taylor among the foremost of these, have argued that only considering the laws of nature in their status of divine commands leads to finding an acceptable theory of obligation in Hobbes. It is important to recognize, however, that this view is the function of some important premises about what may legitimately constitute obligation. It is highly doubtful that Hobbes shared these premises, though, and it is equally questionable whether these premises are as incontrovertible as proponents of the Taylor-Warrender position tend to assume. Specifically, this position rests upon the premise that political obligation must be grounded in moral obligation and in that alone. This must be the case, the argument runs, since political obligation cannot be grounded upon itself; but it cannot be grounded upon the nature of things either, since this would be a derivation of an 'ought' from an 'is.' Therefore, for Taylor and Warrender, the grounds of political obligation must be found in an antecedent moral obligation and in that alone if it is to pass muster as a genuine theory of obligation. These requirements for an acceptable theory of obligation are reflected, for example, where Warrender says: 'If the laws of nature in the State of Nature are not regarded as the commands of God, they may be taken to be merely rational principles of prudence. The atheist, presumably, would have some use for these maxims as they

would be a guide to his preservation, but he could not consider them as laws, and, as we have seen, could not be obliged
by them.'[48]

If one accepts the premises of this argument, the conclusions
follow; and, as stated earlier, Hobbes would have been perfectly pleased for anyone to feel bound to obey the laws of
nature because they were divine dictates. It is not necessary,
however, to construe the nature of obligation so narrowly.
There is no reason that political obligation cannot be grounded
in natural obligation as well as in moral obligation, unless one
insists *a priori* that this is illicit. Such an insistence may reflect a
personal refusal to be obliged by anything other than what one
is willing to consider a moral imperative. This is anyone's
privilege. However, it is conceivable that there are such things
as natural imperatives, as well, and it is perfectly legitimate to
base political imperatives upon these. Warrender's line of
argument tends to obscure Hobbes's belief in the reality of such
natural imperatives and the significant political imperatives
which he believed largely to follow from them.

Because of this narrowing of what constitutes a genuine
theory of obligation, Warrender's depiction of Hobbes is
disturbingly eccentric in the literal sense of that word. In the
first place, the vast energies which Hobbes devoted to demon-
strating the appropriate political implications of an intelligent
self-interest become virtually irrelevant. The essential Hobbes,
in relation to natural law and political obligation, becomes a
fideist, who believed rational theological propositions impossible
but nevertheless grounded a political theory on divine will; all
the psychological propositions become logically unnecessary
enterprises. If these propositions had any relevance to Hobbes's
political theory, by Warrender's standards it was purely to
sustain the possibility of compliance with natural law, possibility being a necessary validating condition of any obligation.[49] It quickly becomes apparent, however, that almost
everything of interest in Hobbes's theory comes under the
heading of validating condition. Included, for example, are

the mandate of the sovereign and what Hobbes holds to be man's overriding instinct for self-preservation. What is left as the grounds of obligation are peculiarly empty and almost purely formal. Finally, under this view, the parallel of natural and political obligation in Hobbes becomes 'coincidental'; Warrender's logical categories require that the two remain chastely separate, and hence one cannot be seen as connected with the other.[50] This interpretation renders purely accidental what Hobbes would certainly have considered his distinctive achievement, namely, the demonstration that duty is not only not incompatible with self-interest, but follows from it.

In some ways, contrary to the assumptions behind the Warrender approach, the derivation of political obligation from natural obligation is even more compelling than a derivation from moral obligation. Therefore, unless one insists *a priori* that only moral imperatives are genuinely obligatory, basing political obligation upon natural imperatives may provide a more satisfactory theory than basing it upon purely moral grounds. An argument which ends in purely moral grounds, for example, is subject to an infinite regress. If the response to the question 'why should I be politically obligated to do such-and-such?' is 'because that is God's will,' one can then ask why he is obliged to obey God's will. This difficulty becomes apparent in the final, relatively sketchy section of Warrender's book. If one asks why he should obey God, Warrender concedes, the answer must be 'just because it is God's will' (not a very satisfactory ultimate basis for a theory of obligation) or else 'because you will be damned if you do not obey.' In the case of the latter answer, however, one has moved away from purely moral grounds to those of ultimate self-interest on a celestial plane. As Warrender himself observes, then, 'the goal of human endeavour throughout the whole of Hobbes's system, is self-preservation and the avoidance of death, either in the immediate and biological sense, or in an ultimate dispensation by God in a second existence where a final ruling is given.'[51] In effect, however, this final location of the grounds of obligation in a second-world self-interest violates the criterion of an acceptable, purely moral, theory of obligation which Warrender earlier established; and if one can do so at the end, why not earlier?

If Hobbes's natural laws are considered in their role as compelling counsel in the service of self-preservation, it becomes apparent once again how Hobbes preserves the formal matrix of the earlier tradition while departing from it substantively. Both in the classical view of natural law and in Hobbes's view it is possible, and perhaps most enlightening, to see the laws of nature as peculiarly compelling hypothetical imperatives. The peculiar compulsion which they possess arises from the virtually unarguable status of the goal upon which they are contingent, namely, the end of *being a man*. That is, natural laws as hypothetical imperatives can be expressed in the form, 'If you are to be a man, then you must do such-and-such.' Since the only apparent alternatives to being a man are being a god, a beast, or a nonentity, the obligations derived upon such a premise are hard to dispute.

Hobbes, then, formally at least, sounds a lot like Cicero in proclaiming natural laws to be dictates of right reason incumbent upon all who wish to be men.[52] The novelty of Hobbes's position, however, which reduces the natural law to counsels of self-preservation, follows from the novelty of his view of what is entailed in being a man. In the classical ontology, 'being' referred to existence in the tension between origin and completion. The dictates of natural law, therefore, were imperatives consequent upon the necessity of reaching fulfillment as a man. Man being 'naturally,' i.e., in his fruition, a social animal, he was naturally subject to political obligations. His natural tendency (*hormē*) toward communal existence implied irreducible political duties which logically could not be evaded if the end (*telos*) was to be reached. For Hobbes, however, as we have seen, being no longer contains this tension between potential and actual, between existence and essence. Hence, 'to be' means merely to persist, as in the model of inertia; and the phrase 'if you are to be a man' means simply 'if you are to survive.' Imperatives for human action premised upon this virtually unarguable end, therefore, become counsels of self-preservation.

At first impression, it might appear that Hobbes, by eliminating the tension from 'being,' has left himself without the ontological basis for retaining any natural imperatives at all. In the classical cosmos natural laws were the imperatives of fulfilled being (actuality) upon aspirant being (potentiality). With the abandonment of the actual–potential, essence–existence setting, there would seem to remain no obligations that could grow from the necessities of a teleological order of nature. If reality is tensionless, then it would seem to follow that a theory of obligation must, as Warrender argues, begin with the moral imperative of divine will or else be no theory of obligation at all, but simply an account of motivation. The alternatives, however, are not as simple as this.

Although nature, in Hobbes's view, is not characterized as the Aristotelian cosmos was by the tension of potential and actual, it does have elements of tension within it. The tension which Hobbes perceives is not vertical, but horizontal; it occurs wholly within the single plane of appetites and aversions which comprise 'natural lust.' Nevertheless, it provides the necessary basis for continuing to perceive the presence of imperatives for human behavior grounded in the nature of things.

This element of tension within Hobbes's nonteleological view of nature Michael Oakeshott tries to express by saying that, for Hobbes, 'there is a radical conflict between the nature of man and the natural condition of mankind.'[53] Specifically, two different components of man's complement of natural inclinations are at war with each other: his natural pridefulness, or vainglory, and his natural inclination to preserve his own life. Both of these drives are natural; both are self-oriented. Yet they are incapable of harmonious coexistence. As Oakeshott observes, in Hobbes's view the human predicament is that 'nature itself is the author of his ruin.'[54]

The phenomenon of natural obligation arises because, while both vainglory and the fear of violent death are natural passions, they are not of equal importance. Both logically and in fact, in Hobbes's view, the aversion to violent death takes precedence over all the other passions. Where it conflicts with them, it must prevail, since self-preservation is the *sine qua non* of satisfying any other natural inclination. 'There can be no contentment but in proceeding,' Hobbes reminds us.[55] Or, to put it in another way, the dead have no pleasures. Violent death is the *summum malum*, as Leo Strauss puts it, and the natural passion engendered by the apprehension of this fact has priority over the other natural passions. Therefore it is this master aversion, the fear of violent death, which is the 'purging' and 'civilizing' emotion[56] that 'brings man to reason'[57] and provides the basis for civil order. The dictates of the natural law are imperatives which follow logically from the overriding necessity to preserve one's life.

Critics such as Warrender and Taylor contend that the laws of nature must be more than prudential maxims for self-preservation of this sort. Hobbes would agree that they can be conceived as more than this, as divine dictates with intrinsic moral status, but they need not be more. Warrender argues that the formula required for the creation of a state is not 'preserve yourself' but 'act so that all men can be preserved, except where this is inconsistent with your own preservation.' 'This,' says Warrender, 'is, of course, an entirely different matter, and a prescriptive principle of this kind could never be derived from the ordinary self-interest of the individual alone.'[58] Hobbes's contention, however, is precisely that such a prescriptive principle can be derived from self-interest. The individual does not wish to accept the admonition to preserve the life of others *per se*, Hobbes agrees, but he is logically forced to do so in order to avoid self-destruction. Only by covenanting submission to a sovereign, who necessarily transcends his own particular interest, can the individual secure the indispensable core of self-interest, the reasonable hope of survival. And of course this cannot be achieved without recognizing and consenting to the self-preservation of other men as well, since they would otherwise not join the pact. What Warrender argues must be an *a priori* transcendent principle of obligation, Hobbes sees as an intrinsically repugnant self-sacrifice necessitated by the absolute horror of the condition of 'meer nature.'[59]

Hobbes's attempt to reconcile self-interest and political obligation is not quite as radical and distinctive in form as it might appear. What is distinctive in Hobbes is the narrowness of his conception of self-interest, a substantive peculiarity which makes the attempted reconciliation so novel and stark. As long as man is conceived of as naturally a social animal, the concept of self-interest contains a barely submerged paradox: the human individual cannot act in his true self-interest if he, acting from motives of immediate advantage, breaks the social ties which permit him to be a man. Because this paradox dissolved in Hobbes, the problem of reconciling self-interest and political obligation becomes considerably more difficult. And this paradox is dissolved by the new conception of nature as a chaos of self-contained, atomistic entities which cohere only through artificial interference. The grounds of 'natural' community are lost; 'meer nature' cannot bind men; therefore, it falls to the sovereign power to do so.

NOTES

1. Aristotle, *Physics*, 2. 1. 192b.
2. Ibid., 3. 1. 200b.
3. Ibid., 3. 1. 201b.
4. Ibid., 2. 4–6.
5. Ibid., 2. 8. 198b.
6. See Friedrich Solmsen, *Aristotle's System of the Physical World* (Ithaca, N.Y.: Cornell University Press, 1960), pp. 91 ff.
7. Aristotle, *Metaphysics*, 1. 3. 984b.
8. Aristotle, *Physics*, 8. 1. 252a.

9. Ibid., 2. 8. 199a.

10. Ibid., 2. 8. 199b.

11. Aristotle, *Politics*, trans. Ernest Barker (London: Oxford University Press, 1946), 1. 2. 1252b.

12. Ibid., 1. 2. 1253a.

13. Ibid.

14. Ibid.

15. Hobbes, *English Works*, 2: 3.

16. Ibid., 2: 2.

17. Ibid., 2: 5.

18. Hobbes, *Leviathan*, p. 103.

19. Ibid., p. 104.

20. Ibid., p. 101.

21. *English Works*, 2: 8.

22. Ibid., 2: 5.

23. *Leviathan*, p. 105.

24. Aristotle, *Physics*, 5. 1. 224b.

25. Descartes, *Rules for Direction*, p. 24.

26. See Hobbes, *English Works*, 1: 69.

27. Ibid.

28. *The Political Theory of Possessive Individualism* (Oxford: Oxford University Press, 1962), p. 18.

29. Ibid., p. 23.

30. Hobbes, Rousseau felt, was among 'those who, in reasoning on the state of nature, always import into it ideas gathered in a state of society' ('A Discourse on the Origin of Inequality,' trans. G. D. H. Cole, Everyman's Library [New York: E. P. Dutton Co.], p. 214).

31. For example in the passage which reads: 'And thus much for the ill condition, which man by meer Nature is actually placed in; though with a possibility to come out of it' (*Leviathan*, p. 106).

32. Hobbes, *Leviathan*, p. 104.

33. *English Works*, 2: 8.

34. *Leviathan*, p. 3.

35. Ibid., p. 41.

36. Ibid., p. 124.

37. Ibid., p. 70.

38. Consider the following examples. 1) economic: 'When he discovered that the raw materials of his product could be synthesized for a fraction of the cost, he quite naturally adopted that procedure'; 2) psychological: 'Repeatedly frustrated in his attempts, the child naturally became quite angry'; 3) biological: 'The blossoms of that plant grow that way naturally'; 4) physical: 'When he heated the air, naturally it expanded.'

39. *The Idea of Nature* (New York: Oxford University Press, 1960).

40. *English Works*, 1: 74.

41. See 'Introduction' to *Leviathan*, pp. lviii–lxi.

42. *Leviathan*, p. 310.

43. Warrender, *The Political Philosophy of Hobbes*, p. 334.

44. 'Therefore between Counsell and Command, one great difference is, that Command is directed to a man's own benefit; and Counsell to the benefit of another man' (*Leviathan*, p. 217).

45. Ibid.

46. 'The Ethical Doctrine of Hobbes,' in Brown, ed., *Hobbes Studies*, p. 49.

47. *Leviathan*, p. 133.

48. Warrender, *The Political Philosophy of Hobbes*, p. 99.

49. For an elaboration of the distinction between the grounds of an obligation and the validating conditions of an obligation, see ibid., pp. 14 ff.

50. 'A coincidence of duty and interest does not imply that they are identical, nor that self-interest is the ground of obligation.' Ibid., p. 277.

51. Warrender, *The Political Philosophy of Hobbes*, p. 308. The parallelism is especially striking here, since damnation in Hobbes's view is not eternal torment but a final, irrevocable death.

52. Hobbes, *English Works*, 2: 13 and 16.

53. Oakeshott, 'Introduction' to *Leviathan*, p. xxxv.

54. Ibid.

55. *English Works*, 4: 33.

56. Oakeshott, 'Introduction' to *Leviathan*, p. xxxvi.

57. Strauss, *The Political Philosophy of Hobbes*, p. 18.

58. Warrender, 'A Reply to Mr. Plamenatz,' in Keith Brown, ed., *Hobbes Studies*, p. 97.

59. A good example of the problem which Hobbes sees as facing man in the state of nature is that faced in international politics by a nation which cannot or will not recognize the right to existence of another nation. Currently, certain of the Arab countries are in this position in relation to Israel. Without recognizing the right of the other to his existence, no nation can negotiate any agreement with its neighbors; and with no agreement, there is no security. This analogy is not perfect, because the binding force of a transcending sovereign power cannot be found in international politics, the nearest functional equivalent being an enforcement pledge by the great powers. The essential lesson is, however, quite manifest: without granting the right of everyone to self-preservation, no one can secure his own continued existence.

5

A New Science and Political Deliverance

'We learn either by induction or by demonstration.' — *Aristotle*

'There is therefore no method by which we find out
the causes of things, but is either compositive or
resolutive, or partly compositive, and partly resolutive.' — *Hobbes*

The basic patterns which Hobbes perceives as characteristic of
nature carry over into his philosophical anthropology. This
permeation of Hobbes's vision of man by his fundamental
cosmological vision is logically quite proper; for man is himself
in Hobbes's view one part of the whole of nature, and he could
therefore justifiably be considered as sharing the fundamental
properties of the natural order. As Hobbes says in the Introduction to the *Leviathan*, man is 'that Rationall and most
excellent work of Nature.'[1]

The Cartesian solution to the problem of where to locate
man in the world of *res extensa* was simply to extrude him from
the natural world altogether. This solution, of course, brings
with it some dilemmas of its own. Having banished the 'ghost'
of thinking substance from the external world, one is hard put
to explain their obvious and intimate interconnection. Such a
radically dualistic formulation never appealed to Hobbes. For
his thoroughly monistic mentality the only option was to
retain the notion of the natural order as a single all-encompassing whole. Anything that was not part of the bodily world
simply did not exist for him. 'For the Universe, being the
Aggregate of all Bodies, there is no reall part thereof that is not
also Body; nor anything properly a Body, that is not also part of
(that Aggregate of all Bodies) the Universe.'[2]

I

This monistic insistence upon the unity of the world, like much of the basic framework of Hobbes's thought, probably was partly due to the heavy component of tacit Aristotelianism which his mind contained. Anyone who reads the Aristotelian arguments against the Platonic conception of the Forms[3] should find a strong formal resemblance to Hobbes's anti-dualistic contentions. Whatever exists, both for Aristotle and for Hobbes, is a part of the world; and the world is a *universe*, not a tenuous conjunction of radically different forms of being such as Ideas and 'sensible things' or extended substance and thinking substance. In the context of this monistic vision, then, a transformation in the fundamental conception of nature exercises a particularly compelling influence over the shape of the conception of *human* nature. Since man is a part of nature in the seamless web of the universe he must share some of its most basic properties and patterns of behavior. There is no escape hatch from the world of nature, no protected area or special status which man could have to exempt him from the forces and realities which govern the rest of the cosmos. Man might be the 'most excellent' of nature's works, to use Hobbes's phrase, but he is one of nature's works nevertheless.

In the context of a nondualistic world view, then, the idea of nature which Hobbes develops has a clear logical bearing upon his image of man. Some of the ways in which this bearing is manifested will be examined in the following pages. Before doing so, however, it is worth noting that the conception of human nature which emerges will have an obvious and profound impact upon the political prescriptions which Hobbes sees as the final fruit of his inquiry. For the political order is a product of which man is both the architect (the immediate, contingent architect, at least) and the inhabitant. Therefore, the shape of the polis must be determined by reference to both man's needs and his capabilities: it is determined by his needs as the inhabitant and by his capabilities as the architect. Any political program which does not rest firmly upon a realistic assessment of these key components of human nature, then, is doomed to futility. It is for this reason that the classical pattern of political theorizing involves centrally the binding together of sociology and philosophical anthropology. To this pattern Hobbes is no exception, both because he was a realist who had no use for what he held to be futile or self-defeating exertions and because he was quite classical in his philosophical orientation, though not in his philosophical substance.

Writers in the seventeenth century generated some rather strange and striking anthropological views. Perhaps the most striking and influential of these, and the most persistently problematic in the area of epistemology, is the Cartesian view of what Gilbert Ryle has termed the 'ghost in the machine.' Immersed, like Descartes, in the radical transformation of the classical conception of the cosmos, Hobbes also finds it necessary to produce a new model of human behavior to replace the one which had been predicated upon the earlier cosmology. In response to this need, Hobbes produces his own unique, and stunningly modern, conception of man.

The two basic sides of man, and therefore the two basic components of any model of his basic nature, are his cognitive and intellectual processes and his affective behavior—his reason and his emotion. These two components, though closely interrelated, are nonetheless distinguishable aspects of the whole of human activity. The critical foundations of a model of man, then, arise in response to the questions 'what does it mean to be *homo sapiens*, the *knowing* animal?' and 'what are the basic motivations in human action?' To each of these critical questions, Hobbes provides his own distinctive answer. To know, he says, is to compute; and the fundamental motivating forces of human action are the vain desire for 'precellence' and the irreducible necessity for self-preservation. In the context of an open and insecure world, then, the composite view of man which emerges is that of a vain, power-hungry, and anxious 'computer.'

Each of these facets of human behavior which Hobbes combines into his inimitable view of man grows in part from his unflinching and often acidic observations of life around him. Like la Rochefoucauld, Hobbes seems ever attuned to perceive the admixture of egoism in virtually every human deed. He seems to take a perverse satisfaction in rooting even the most altruistic of human actions in the quest for power which he perceives to be universal. These autonomous interpretative observations of men and manners, in short, were obviously, as D. H. Robertson and others have observed, supremely important sources of the systematic conception of human nature which Hobbes ultimately articulated. Yet it is also true that this systematic view of human nature was very firmly rooted in his fundamental cosmological vision. The basic focal paradigm of inertial motion which shapes the Hobbesian conception of nature proceeds through this channel to shape his doctrine of man. The two basic sides of man, his reason and his passions, are designated by Hobbes as 'the principal parts of Nature.'[4] The portrait of mankind which Hobbes paints for us, then, is not merely a composite of his *ad hoc* observations of human behavior, but is also an expression of those fundamental attributes of the cosmos which man, the natural creature, shares with the rest of the natural world. For example, Hobbes's belief that men seek their own self-interest is not simply a statistical generalization—a 'general tendency' statement—adduced purely from untheoretical observation. It instead has the status of a universal tendency ontologically grounded in the essential properties of nature.[5]

This systematic and ontologically grounded vision of human nature, needs, and capabilities which Hobbes develops once again replicates the basic pattern of a radically transformed Aristotelianism which characterizes his whole philosophy. The conception of human cognitive powers which Hobbes arrives at is essentially the Aristotelian model of demonstrative science set into the context of nominalist premises. The forms of Aristotelian inquiry are retained, even though the realist assumptions which Aristotle (with good cause) felt necessary to keep the enterprise viable are rejected. And the theoretical conception of human affectivity and motivation which Hobbes develops adopts the Aristotelian model of natural tendency (*hormē*), but transforms it radically by stripping away its setting in teleology. We shall look at each in turn—the cognitive in this chapter and the affective in the following chapter.

First, let us consider the case of Hobbesian 'science.' In Aristotelian thought, 'not only art but knowledge imitates nature.'[6] The same is true in Hobbes, as we might expect, since he tacitly accepts most of the formal patterns of Aristotelian thought. Since, however, the substantive model of nature which he deems indicated by Galileo's discoveries is different from the substance of Aristotelian nature, Hobbes's model of human cognition undergoes a parallel change. In both Hobbes and Aristotle science is depicted as basically demonstrative, proceeding from clearly apprehended premises codified in definitions to demonstrated conclusion through syllogistic reason. The actual meaning of this pattern of scientific inquiry is quite different, however, in Hobbes's indefinite and nominalist world from what it is in the finite and realistic world of Aristotle.

Aristotelian science is composed of the processes of demonstration and induction. The former proceeds from the universal to the particular, while the latter moves from the particular to the universal. These processes, of course, require bases from which to begin. These starting points for scientific discourse are accurate definitions, apprehensions of the essential nature of the genus or subject matter under consideration. Science, in fact, depends for Aristotle upon the possibility of univocal predication—upon things existing in such a way that they may be defined precisely and distinctively. The means by which man could reach this apprehension of essential nature was his *nous*, his intuitive capacity to grasp the basic structure of the entities which comprise the cosmos. And this capacity, in turn, is possible simply because the senses are capable, through time, of accurately distinguishing the universal patterns which are manifested in the recurrence of particulars. Upon this kind of experience, then, man, the rational animal, could construct his edifice of scientific knowledge. When man reached this kind of knowledge, moreover, 'knowledge of the reasoned fact,' he possessed knowledge of the fundamental causes at work, as well.[7]

Several observations need to be made about this epistemological account of Aristotle. In the first place, this account of the process of knowing contains irreducible components of rationalism, empiricism, and intuitionism. Aristotle was neither a rationalist, nor an empiricist, nor an intuitionist in any simple and exclusive sense, then, but was a combination of all three. Each performed one function within his overall account of knowledge; none served him as an exclusive mode of knowing. It is the specific functions of the different components and their interrelationship that is essential to his method. This point is worth emphasizing in light of recurrent controversies as to whether Aristotle was an empiricist or a rationalist. Clearly he was both, in a sense, and neither in another sense. Simple modern labels serve more to distort than to illuminate his approach.

Second, it is essential to realize how deeply embedded in and dependent upon his ontological beliefs Aristotle's epistemological program was. As Marjorie Grene aptly observes: 'Aristotle's logic is not a pure logic, a system valid for "all possible worlds," like the formal systems envisaged by Leibniz. It is an analysis of the kind of discourse valid for expressing man's knowledge of this one, unique universe.'[8]

Aristotelian science is a closed system of discourse, applicable fully only to a universe which is itself closed—i.e., finite. The furniture of the universe must be subject to real definition if it is to be known, and it can be defined in univocal and real fashion only if it is itself finite.[9]

Hobbes's conception of the nature and powers of human reason are not always wholly clear and consistent.[10] However, there is a discernible basic pattern to his account of what being a rational animal entails, and that pattern can be characterized as an adaptation of the fundamentals of Aristotelian methodology to a nominalist universe. The key components of Aristotelian science are replicated in Hobbes's account of knowledge, but they become radically transformed by the new setting. The viability of this attempt on the part of Hobbes is open to serious question, of course; for Aristotelian method was structured from the outset to be uniquely applicable to the Aristotelian cosmos. Hobbes, nevertheless, inspired to a significant extent by the Paduan school of Italian Aristotelians, tries to accomplish the necessary adaptation; and, however unsuccessful the attempt is ultimately, it has some notable consequences for the political uses of reason.

Both Hobbes and Aristotle scatter their methodological formulations throughout their writings. However, Aristotle's explicit consideration of the functions and capabilities of human reason appear most centrally in his *Organon*, the treatises on logic, reaching their apex in the *Posterior Analytics*. Hobbes's most systematic presentation of the same topic appears in Part One of *De Corpore*. If these two texts are examined carefully together, it becomes possible to perceive once again, this time in the treatment of human reason, the pattern we have indicated throughout as characteristic of Hobbes's work, namely, the pattern of radical transformation of Aristotelian doctrine, with the content of the basic forms changed in the attempt to apply them to the conception of reality which informs the seventeenth century.

To begin with, Hobbes asserts like Aristotle that the end of science is the certain knowledge of the causes and effects of things which are 'generated.' It is to be demonstrated knowledge, reached by a process of logical reasoning from first premises to demonstrated conclusion. Hobbes, who uses the terms philosophy and science interchangeably, puts it this way: 'Philosophy is such knowledge of effects or appearances, as we acquire by true ratiocination from the knowledge we have first of their causes or generation: And again, of such causes or generations as may be from knowing first their effects.'[11] For Aristotle, similarly, the end of scientific inquiry was the acquisition of certain knowledge of necessary causes; and demonstrative reason played a key part in reaching this end.

> We suppose ourselves to possess unqualified scientific knowledge of a thing, as opposed to knowing it in the accidental way in which the sophist knows, when we think that we know the cause on which the fact depends, as the cause of that fact and of no other, and, further, that the fact could not be other than it is. . . .
> . . . at all events we do know by demonstration. By demonstration I mean a syllogism productive of scientific knowledge.[12]

Hobbes likewise echoes the Aristotelian format as he asserts that scientific knowledge, demonstrative as it is, cannot be circular. That is, one cannot begin anywhere in the series of propositions that constitute a scientific argument as he could legitimately do if the pattern of scientific inquiry were logically circular. 'For we may not, as in a circle, begin the handling of a science from what point we please. There is a certain clue of reason, whose beginning is in the dark; but by the benefit of whose conduct, we are led as it were by the hand into the clearest light.'[13] The Aristotelian argument against the belief that 'demonstration may be circular and reciprocal' may be found in Book 1, Chapter 3, of the *Posterior Analytics*.[14]

For both Hobbes and Aristotle, then, scientific knowledge is a linear progression to demonstrated conclusions about cause and effect. The next problem which logically must be confronted is: what are the starting points for this linear pattern of knowledge? Where does scientific knowing have the autonomous grounds which prevent it from being circular? Obviously, it is requisite for the scientist to begin with premises. Aristotle captures this clear logical necessity, saying, 'the required ground of our knowledge of a fact is the possession of such a syllogism as we call demonstration, and the ground of the syllogism is the facts constituting its premises.'[15]

Here, with a consideration of the nature, source, warrant, and functions of these scientific premises we reach the real crux of the scientific methodology, of the conception of human reason, of both Hobbes and Aristotle. (Hobbes uses the terms 'principles' or 'primary propositions' or 'universal' principles or propositions to signify these premises; but he is referring to precisely the same thing as far as their logical and methodological function is concerned.) For these premises, or first principles, support the whole burden of scientific certainty. The process of syllogistic reason, of computation as Hobbes calls it, is only as good as its premises. Those who begin with faulty premises, as Hobbes so graphically puts it 'at last finding the error visible, and not mistrusting their first grounds, know not which way to cleere themselves; but spend time in fluttering over their books; as bird that entering by the chimney, and finding themselves inclosed in a chamber, flutter at the false light of a glass window, for want of wit to consider which way they came in.'[16] Therefore, for science to exist, true premises must be obtainable. The necessity of possessing true premises for science —'the reckoning of consequences,' as Hobbes puts it—to begin is reflected in Aristotle's clear statement of the burden these first principles must carry: 'The premises of demonstrated knowledge must be true, primary, immediate, better known than and prior to the conclusion, which is further related to them as effect to cause. Unless these conditions are satisfied, the basic truths will not be appropriate to the conclusion. Syllogism there may be without these conditions, but such syllogism, not being productive of scientific knowledge, will not be demonstration.'[17]

The apprehension of these necessary premises, or primary propositions, then, may be characterized as the foundations of scientific knowledge, both for Hobbes and for the Aristotelian account which he attempts to adapt and supersede. Upon their validity the whole superstructure of scientific conclusions depends. Given the lack of circularity of scientific knowledge in both the Hobbesian and Aristotelian framework, moreover, these critical underpinnings of the whole enterprise must themselves be recognized as not subject to demonstration. Aristotle writes: 'Knowledge of the immediate premises is independent of demonstration. The necessity of this is obvious; for since we must know the prior premises from which the demonstration is drawn, and since the regress must end in immediate truths, those truths must be indemonstrable.'[18] Hobbes follows this pattern quite closely, once again, saying that universal principles 'because they are principles cannot be demonstrated.'[19]

What, then, are these premises, these primary propositions, which are indemonstrable, but upon which all else depends? The answer, once more is the same for Hobbes as for Aristotle: the propositions which serve as the fundamental premises of scientific demonstration are definitions. The Aristotelian expression of this view runs as follows: 'Moreover, the basic premises of demonstrations are definitions, and it has already been shown that these will be found indemonstrable; either the basic premises will be demonstrable and will depend on prior premises, and the regress will be endless; or the primary truths will be indemonstrable definitions.'[20] The comparable passage in Hobbes states: 'Now primary propositions are nothing but definitions, or parts of definitions, and these only are the principles of demonstration.'[21] And later Hobbes asserts that demonstration 'begins from primary or most universal propositions, which are manifest of themselves, and proceeds by a perpetual composition of propositions into syllogisms, till at last the learner understands the truth of the conclusion sought after. . . . such principles are nothing but definitions.'[22] In fact, Hobbes asserts, 'the only way to know is by definition.'[23]

Hobbes, then, continues to follow the Aristotelian tradition in which he had been instructed: from the insistence upon the demonstrative character of scientific knowledge, through the postulation of indemonstrable premises which are related in a cause–effect way to the conclusions, to the identification of these premises with definitions. The next question which logically arises, however, is the problem 'what are these definitions?' And in his response to this substantive question, Hobbes departs from the traditional Aristotelian answer. Once again we find a radical transformation in content occurring at a crucial point within the context of persistent formal parallelism. And once again, this transformation is governed by the need to adapt the overall paradigm to the structural features of the new cosmos. Hobbes, pursuing the Aristotelian epistemological format, attributes critical significance to the act of definition, but defining something in a world of Body cannot be the same thing as defining something in a world of substances.

In the Aristotelian world of finite, universal forms, the definition of an entity was the specification of the unique 'this-ness' which made the entity what it was and which distinguished it from all other entities. The act of definition is possible, in Aristotle's view only a) because nature is the way it is—i.e., because the world is composed of 'definite things characterized by definite structures and definite life-histories, things which group themselves naturally according to these structures and processes, so that the world, in itself, displays the finitude essential to knowledge';[24] and b) because the human mind, as itself a product of nature, possesses the capability of clearly perceiving these substantive patterns. The sublime confidence in the inherent capacity of the human mind was, as Grene astutely observes, more than likely the result of Aristotle's own experience as a biologist. That is, his biological investigations depended upon a prior identification of a particular species as being what it was and not another species. Aristotle experienced little difficulty in perceiving the pattern and properties of a species in recurrent individual specimens and in distinguishing one species from another; and it was therefore not surprising that he generalized this discriminative capacity of the practicing biologist into his systematic epistemology.[25]

It follows from the above account that Aristotle considered the act of definition to be a specification of the essence of a particular thing. 'Definition is of the essential nature or being of something.'[26] Hobbes, however, must give a different account of what is involved in a definition, since the ontological context of his epistemology has no essences in it. Having conflated all heterogeneous substances into a single substance—i.e., Body— Hobbes cannot view definition as an account of substantive boundary lines. He recognizes this quite clearly and affirms it explicitly:

> this is manifest, that genus, species, definition, etc. are names of words and names only; and therefore to put genus and species for things, and definition for the nature of any thing, as the writers of metaphysics have done, is not right, seeing they be only significations of what we think of the nature of things.
>
> Names have their constitution, not from the species of things, but from the will and consent of men.
>
> For definition is not the essence of any thing, but a speech signifying what we conceive of the essence thereof; and so also not whiteness itself, but the word whiteness, is a genus, or a universal name.[27]

If definitions, as conceived in the Aristotelian tradition, are not representations of the essence of any thing, what are they? Hobbes answers that they are explications of names.[28] These explications may take one of two forms, depending upon the type of name in question. If it is a compound name, that is, a name composed of more universal names (as the name 'man' may be said to be compounded of the names 'rational,' 'body,' 'animated,' and so on), then the definition will consist of resolving that compound name into its simple and universal constituents. If the name is itself 'the most universal in its kind,' then the definition is a predication of different words which signify exactly the same thing. A definition, then, concludes Hobbes, is 'a proposition, whose predicate resolves the subject, when it may; and when it may not, it exemplifies the same.'[29]

This account of definitions, of course, takes place in a resolutely nominalist context, where names are 'taken at pleasure'; and definitions therefore are 'truths constituted arbitrarily by the inventors of speech.'[30] Hobbes's account of naming and definitions is ultimately quite weak, especially considering the enormous burden which they carry.[31] It is not really clear what the formal requisites are of a definition which cannot resolve, because the name in question refers to a universal thing, but instead can only be 'such circumlocution as best explicateth the force of that name.'[32] Nor is it made clear what the standards of right definition are in a nominalist context.[33] What is clear is that Hobbes's account of definition of compound names (and most definitions would be of this sort) is a direct reflection of his ontological departure from the Aristotelian tradition: namely, to ask for the nature of a thing means to ask for its *component parts* rather than for the *formal whole* it represents. This crucial difference receives systematic expression in Hobbes's characterization of the modes of scientific inquiry. It is also clear that, with all their deficiencies, Hobbesian definitions continue to perform absolutely critical functions in his account of human knowledge, just as essential definitions did in Aristotelian epistemology. These definitions are the source of all knowledge, the beginning of science, the first principles of reason, and the subject matter of *philosophia prima*.[34]

Moreover, it is also notable that Hobbes preserves largely formally intact, in his transformed ontological context, the Aristotelian account of the warrant for accreditation of definitional primary propositions and of the process of apprehending them.

In both Hobbes's and Aristotle's accounts of the procedural means of reaching the universal definitive principles from which all scientific knowledge must be derived the same basic pattern is present. The inquiry into first principles begins with sensation. Next, recurrent images of the senses result in remembrance. The accumulation of memories become experience. Experience leads to the apprehension of first principles. And finally, reasoning from these principles produces a kind of artificial experience which is science. The Aristotelian exposition of this process is most cogently expounded in the final chapter of the *Posterior Analytics*; however, the basic sequence of sense–memory–experience–first principles–science may be seen in the following passage: 'So out of sense-perception comes to be what we call memory, and out of frequently repeated memories of the same thing develops experience; for a number of memories constitute a single experience. From experience again—i.e., from the universal now stabilized in its entirety within the soul, the one beside the many which is a single identity within them all—originate the skill of the craftsman and the knowledge of the man of science, skill in the sphere of coming to be and science in the sphere of being.'[35]

Hobbes's account of the natural history of science, his genetic epistemology as it were, is virtually identical to Aristotle's, Like Aristotle, Hobbes sees the origins of all knowledge in sensation. 'The first beginnings, therefore, of knowledge, are the phantasms of sense and imagination.'[36] Later in the same volume, he elaborates and begins to link the original sense-impressions to the phenomenon of memory, which itself plays a significant role in the rise of scientific knowledge: 'we must needs acknowledge sense to be the principle by which we know those principles, and that all the knowledge we have is derived from it. And as for the causes of sense, we cannot begin our search of them from any other phenomenon than that of sense itself. But you will say, by what sense shall we take notice of sense? I answer, by sense itself, namely, by the memory which for some time remains in us of things sensible, though they themselves pass away.'[37] The patterns of the senses, perpetuated by memory to the point that the recurrence of general patterns may be recognized, turns into experience; and science itself is but one mode of knowing contingent upon this experience. This linkage of memory, experience, and science, the final part of the Aristotelian formal sequence of the generation of scientific knowing, is reflected in *De Homine*:

By this we may understand, there be two kinds of knowledge, whereof the one is nothing else but sense, or knowledge original, . . . and remembrance of the same; the other is called science. . . . Both of these sorts are but experience; the former being the experience of the effects of things that work upon us from without; and the latter experience men have from the proper use of names in language: and all experience being, as I have said, but remembrance, all knowledge is remembrance: and of the former, the register we keep in books, is called history; but the registers of the latter are called the sciences.[38]

The formal parallelism between Hobbes and the Aristotelian tradition extends from the process by which first principles are apprehended to the warrant for belief in them. Hobbes, like Aristotle, feels that it is the nature of first principles to command assent by the very power, immediacy, and indubitability with which they present themselves to the human mind. If scientific knowledge is to be certain, the originative principles of scientific demonstration must be certain; but since the warrant of the principles of demonstration cannot be itself demonstrative (if circularity is to be avoided), the warrant must be the capacity of the principles to exhibit themselves as necessary, self-evident, and indubitable truths.

For those who are accustomed to hearing Aristotle praised for his resolutely empirical methodology, the fact that he finally based his claim for scientific validity upon such an aprioristic argument may seem strange. It is nevertheless the case. For while Aristotle insisted upon careful empirical observation and equally careful logical demonstration as the principal components of his scientific procedure, the critical linchpin of the whole system was the presumption that the human mind could accurately perceive first principles by intuition (*nous*). Intuition, he said in the concluding remarks of the *Posterior Analytics*, was 'the originative source of scientific knowledge.'[39] And the first principles grasped by intuition must be self-evident: 'Things are true and primary which are believed on the strength not of anything else but of themselves: for in regard to the first principles of science it is improper to ask any further for the why and wherefore of them; each of the first principles should command belief in and by itself.'[40]

Hobbes's conclusions about the self-evidencing nature of first principles as their warrant for our acceptance of them is essentially the same. A true definition, he asserts, will command assent through its undeniable clarity: 'the nature of a definition consists in this, that it exhibit a clear idea of the thing defined; and principles are either known by themselves, or else they are not principles.'[41] The reliance of Hobbes upon 'clear and distinct ideas' as the ultimate criterion for the acceptance of basic truths, of the fundamental premises of scientific demonstration, is not too surprising in historical context. The seventeenth century, in its predominant intellectual style, was almost uniquely convinced of the power and presence of self-evident truths. But this calm confidence in the powers of intuitive reason was merely an accentuation of a pattern already there in the Greek conception of *nous*.[42] What is strikingly different from the Aristotelian characterization of intuitive perception of self-evident premises is the substance of what is seen to be self-evident. For Aristotle, intuitive perception was of universal gestalts, patterns of being such as biological species, that seemed to be perenially recurrent entities in a cosmos made up of entities. For Hobbes, as for most of the seventeenth century, intuition was of the universal components, the irreducible constituent parts of a substantively homogeneous universe.

It is on the basis of this crucial underlying substantive change, which is nevertheless placed within the persistent formal context of Aristotelian epistemology, that Hobbes arrives at the heart of his conception of human reason and at his reflexive account of his own methodology. Apart from its intuitive powers, by which it is capable of apprehending self-evident premises clearly presented, human reason consists of two basic intellectual operations: the first is resolution, the method of analytical reason, and the other is composition, the method of synthetical reason. Together, these two mental operations comprise the method of science, which consists of relating causes and effects. 'There is therefore no method, by which we find out the causes of things, but is either compositive or resolutive, or partly compositive, and partly resolutive. And the resolutive is commonly called analytical method, as the compositive is called synthetical.'[43]

The characterization of the two component operations of scientific method as composition and resolution are manifestations of Hobbes's mathematico-mechanical conception of reason. For Hobbes, to reason is to reckon and to reckon is to compute.[44] The sum and substance of science, then, is computation, and science is conceived as a form of applied mathematics which can be adapted to any subject matter which is 'capable of composition and resolution.'[45] In arithmetic one adds and subtracts, multiplies and divides numbers. In geometry, the same operations are performed on lines, figures, angles, and so on. In logic, one adds and subtracts the consequences of words. And in law and politics, one reckons the empirical and logical consequences of laws and the components of human action. 'In summe,' concludes Hobbes, 'in what matter soever there is place for addition and subtraction, there is also place for Reason; and where these have no place, there Reason has nothing at all to do.'[46]

It is clear that this is a model of human reason which could only be held by someone deeply infatuated with the power and accuracy of mathematical reason and heavily committed to a mechanistic conception of the world. For, on this model, knowledge comes about through a kind of intellectual tinkering: the mind takes things apart and puts them back together like a repairman working on a clock. In this way, it reaches an understanding of the subject-matter. The Aristotelian mind, living in a biological cosmos of intelligible species, gestalts,

K

would find such an account of scientific reason peculiar indeed.

Nevertheless, here again Hobbes has fashioned his own philosophical paradigm, this time in the interpretation of cognition, by adapting the traditional Aristotelian paradigm to the demands of his radically new and different ontology. It is fascinating to realize that *composition* and *resolution* are Aristotelian *demonstration* and *induction* placed in a nominalist setting, and thereby transfigured.

Consider first the formally congruent pair of induction and resolution. As Aristotle said, and Hobbes repeats, some things are more known to us and others more known to nature.[47] What is better known to us as men is what we can perceive with our senses, and that is the singular individual thing. What is better known to nature is the universal (for Hobbes, the universals) inherent in this singular whole. The function of resolution for Hobbes is the same as the function of induction for Aristotle, namely, to move from the sense-apprehended singular whole to that which is universal in it. Aristotle assigned this task to induction in the *Posterior Analytics*: 'Thus it is clear that we must get to know the primary premises by induction; for the method by which even sense-perception implants the universal is inductive.'[48]

Since he remains an Aristotelian in his formal epistemological program, Hobbes must specify a type of intellectual operation to accomplish this same critical function of induction. That is, since he conceives of science as demonstrative, he must explain how the primary premises of scientific demonstration are discerned. For Hobbes, as for Aristotle, moreover, the only appropriate premises for a demonstrative science are universal principles. Therefore, some means must be provided for the apprehension of universals, such as Aristotle provided in his account of induction.

Aristotelian induction and Hobbesian resolution, then, are formally and functionally congruent. They accomplish the same thing for science—the apprehension of premises of demonstration—and they accomplish this in the same way, i.e., by moving from the sense-perceived particular to that which is universal in it. The transformation of induction into resolution, or analysis, is necessitated in Hobbes by the radically different substantive subject-matter upon which it must work. Or, to put it another way, induction becomes resolution because the underlying conception of what it is that is universal has been so radically altered. Both induction and resolution have the purpose of knowing universals, but in the heterogeneous and finite cosmos of Aristotle such knowledge is of the essence while in the homogeneous and open universe of Hobbes such knowledge is of the universal parts or components. The apprehension of the universal essence which is 'in' the sense-perceived particular is, in Aristotelian epistemology, a kind of consolidation of a gestalt. The apprehension of the universal parts which are 'in' the sense-perceived singular whole becomes, in Hobbes's epistemology, a kind of intellectual dismantling of the complex whole into its simple and universal components.

In the chapter 'Of Method' in *De Corpore*, Hobbes elaborates his conception of the purposes and process of resolution in a passage worth citing in some detail, since it illustrates rather clearly the principal features pointed out above.

> But to those that search after science indefinitely, which consists in the knowledge of the causes of all things, as far forth as it may be attained, (and the causes of singular things are compounded of the causes of universal or simple things) it is necessary that they know the causes of universal things, or of such accidents as are common to all bodies, that is, to all matter, before they can know the causes of singular things, that is, of those accidents by which one thing is distinguished from another. And, again, they must know what those universal things are, before they can know their causes. Moreover, seeing universal things are contained in the nature of singular things, the knowledge of them is to be acquired by reason,

that is, by resolution. For example, if there be propounded a conception or idea of some singular thing, as of a square, this square is to be resolved into a plain, terminated with a certain number of equal and straight lines and right angles. For by this resolution we have these things universal or agreeable to all matter, namely, line, plain (which contains superficies), terminated, angle, straightness, rectitude, and equality; and if we can find out the causes of these, we may compound them altogether into the cause of a square. Again, if any man propound to himself the conception of gold, he may, by resolving, come to the ideas of solid, visible, heavy, . . . and many other more universal than gold itself; and these he may resolve again, till he come to such things as are most universal. And in this manner, by resolving continually, we may come to know what those things are, whose causes being first known severally, and afterwards compounded, bring us to the knowledge of singular things. I conclude, therefore, that the method of attaining to the universal knowledge of things, is purely analytical.[49]

The second congruent pair is that of Aristotelian demonstration and Hobbesian composition. Both of these intellectual operations begin with the necessary and universal principles provided by induction/resolution. Moreover, Hobbes follows in the Aristotelian formal pattern by postulating that the universal principles contain within them an indication of the definitive causal forces at work.[50] Therefore, demonstration/ composition is a process of drawing out the logical consequences of the universal premises; and, because these premises contain the cause, this process is seen as drawing out the causal consequences at the same time. In both Aristotle and Hobbes, then, the method of demonstration consists of moving from the universal cause to the particular effect. 'Demonstration,' Aristotle wrote, 'develops from universals' and 'is syllogism which proves the cause,'[51] Hobbes concurs: 'The end of science is the demonstration of the causes and generations of things; which if they be not in the definitions, they cannot be found in the conclusion of the first syllogism, that is made from those definitions; and if they be not in the first conclusion, they will not be found in any further conclusion deduced from that; and, therefore, by proceeding in this manner, we shall never come to science; which is against the scope and intention of demonstration.'[52]

Hobbes's formal characterization of compositive, synthetical reason, then, exhibits the same formal pattern and performs the same methodological functions as Aristotelian demonstration. It 'begins from primary or most universal propositions, which are manifest of themselves, and proceeds by a perpetual composition of propositions into syllogisms, till at last the learner understand the truth of the conclusion sought after.'[53] The novelty of the Hobbesian account of demonstration as a process of composition stems, once more, from the adaptation of this basic process to the setting of his novel ontology. In the first place, the transformation of the notion of universals into 'accidents common to all bodies' turns the causal force of the universals into purely efficient causality. And second, since the universals are envisaged as component elements rather than essences, the demonstrative movement from the universal to the particular involves a kind of putting back together of the particular complex whole out of the universal parts which were uncovered by analytical reason.

Before considering the specifically political applications and implications of Hobbes's conception of the nature and powers of human reason, a summary recapitulation of the argument might be in order. Aristotle's and Hobbes's epistemological reflections are not easily digestible and the coherence of the course we have followed to this point may not be easily perceived. The following chart, therefore, may be helpful as a sketchy overview of the structure of Hobbes's scientific methodology and its relationship to the Aristotelian tradition from which he begins.

COMPARISON OF THE STRUCTURE OF SCIENTIFIC
REASON IN HOBBES AND ARISTOTLE

Epistemological task or category	Aristotle	Hobbes
Nature of science/philosophy	Knowledge of necessary cause/consequence	Same as Aristotle
Form of science	Linear, not circular	Same
Scientific premises	Essential definitions containing cause	Nominal definitions containing cause
Universal principles (primary definitions, premises)	Substances, essences	Parts, components (motion and extension)
Process of moving to premises/universal principles	Induction (consolidation of gestalt of species)	Resolution (analyzing particular into universal component elements)
Pathway of induction/ resolution	Sense to memory to experience to perception of universal (from particular to universal)	Same
Apprehension of first principles	Noetic intuition	Mathematical intuition
Warrant of first principles	Indubitability, necessity, exhibition of clear and distinct idea	Same
Discovery of necessary effects/consequences	Demonstration by syllogism (from universal to particular)	Composition, synthesis by syllogistic computation (from universal to particular)
Scope of demonstration	Confined to a single genus in a cosmos of heterogeneous substanecs	Open in a universe of homogeneous body

This chart reflects the basic pattern which I have been seeking to establish: that Hobbes's model of human reason is structurally analogous to Aristotle's epistemological model, with transformations effected as necessary to adapt the model to the infinite, mathematicized universe of the seventeenth century.

Hobbes's account of human reason has a direct bearing upon his political theory in a number of ways. For example, this model of scientific method serves as reflexive elucidation of his own political analysis as he conceives it. That is, his own civil philosophy is depicted as a highly significant fruit of the pattern of inquiry he describes. In his examination of 'politique bodies,' Hobbes feels, he has pursued the proper course of a demonstrative science, from the particular presented to the senses back by 'resolving continually' to the universal principles behind them and from there by composition to the finished construct of the *Leviathan*. In the preface to *De Cive*, Hobbes outlines how his approach to civil philosophy embodies the resolutive-compositive method.

> Concerning my method, . . . I took my beginning from the very matter of civil government, and thence proceeded to its generation and form, and the first beginning of justice. For everything is best understood by its constitutive causes. For as in a watch, or some such small engine, the matter, figure, and motion of the wheels cannot be well known, except it be taken insunder and viewed in parts; so to make a more curious search into the rights of states and duties of subjects, it is necessary, I say, not to take them insunder, but yet that they be so considered as if they were dissolved.[54]

Beginning from perception of the particular as it presents itself to the senses — in the context of civil philosophy, the particular being society as it presently is, the empirical political world — the civil philosopher must resolve it into its universal components. Having discovered these universal components —

in the context of civil philosophy, these components are the natural passions and capabilities of man—the civil philosopher has found the nature, the unvarnished natural universal parts, of social existence. In other words, through the process of resolution, analytical reason, one finds the state of nature. And on the basis of the universal principles which Hobbes feels he uncovers about natural passion, the human mode of that universal cause, motion, he depicts that state of nature as a state of war. 'The foundation therefore which I have laid, standing firm, I demonstrate, in the first place, that the state of men without civil society, which state we may properly call the state of nature, is nothing else but a mere war of all against all.'[55]

The final step of the method in the setting of civil philosophy, then, becomes to recompose the society out of these natural parts—to demonstrate the consequences of the causal component principles for the effect, the complex whole, the state. 'These grounds thus laid, I show further what civil government, and the supreme power in it, and the divers kinds of it are; by what rights particular men, who intend to constitute this civil government, must so necessarily transfer from themselves on the supreme power, whether it be one man or an assembly of men, that, except they do so, it will evidently appear to be no civil government, but the rights which all men have to all things, that is, the rights of war still remain.'[56] This process of social reconstruction Hobbes delineates in the section on 'Dominion' in *De Cive*, and Part 2 of the *Leviathan*.

Hobbes's claim that he has produced his civil philosophy by a process of analytical resolution to the natural and universal principles followed by a recomposition to the reconstructed whole, the *Leviathan*, raises an immediate problem: namely, how can he arrive at a conclusion which differs from his starting point? That is, how can the method of resolution-composition be creative? If you take something apart and put it back together again, must you not arrive back where you started, perhaps with a greater understanding of your subject-matter but nevertheless at the same place? This objection raises an important issue, for what is ultimately at stake here is the whole problem of the relationship between description and prescription in Hobbes's thought. Upon the success of his method in coming up with a political whole at the end of his inquiry which is something different from and better than the political situation from which he started rests Hobbes's claim for his fundamental accomplishment, i.e., to produce prescriptions for political action which will command assent from all who understand the natural principles he uncovers.[57]

Hobbes, it must be said, never gives this problem the explicit attention it deserves or even requires. Any attempt to characterize his implicit conception of how the method of resolution-composition could be creative, could end with a different 'whole' from that which one began by 'resolving,' must necessarily be somewhat speculative. With that caveat, I think we could suppose that Hobbes had in mind something like the following argument. The present political situation from which I begin my analysis, he might say, is rather like the situation of a broken watch. The watch repairman, when he comes to fix it, must take it apart and put it back together properly, with the parts arranged this time in accordance with their nature. In the same way, Hobbes would argue, I have come upon a society broken and disordered by civil strife, taken it apart into its fundamental constituent parts, and imaginatively recomposed it into the ordered whole which is consonant with the nature of those parts. This analogy, of course, presumes the validity of designating the situation from which Hobbes begins as somehow 'broken,' but Hobbes feels this is no problem; the natural passions of all men would affirm the unsatisfactoriness of the condition of civil war. Men have not arrived in this sad state because they wanted to be in it, even though they might have gotten there 'naturally.' They got there because of a defect in their understanding. 'The cause of war,' Hobbes asserts, 'is not that men are *willing* to have it; for the will has nothing for object but good' but rather 'that men *know not* the *causes* neither of war nor peace.'[58]

Perhaps a better analogy even than that of the broken clock and the repairman—an image to which Hobbes is strongly attuned—is the analogy of the chess game played by a novice and criticized by a master, suggested by J. W. N. Watkins.[59] In this analogy the novice is mankind in general, the master is Hobbes, and the game itself represents the world of political action. Man, in this analogy, is like a chess novice who, making each move on the basis of what seemed natural at the time, eventually finds himself in a deteriorating strategic situation that ends in his checkmate. Each individual move may have seemed like a good idea at the time, to take the opponent's bishop, to put his king in the corner for protection, and so on. But the composite of the individual moves which seemed right at the time turns out to be disaster. How could this happen? He thought he knew everything he needed to know—how each piece moved, the object of the game, and so on—but he reached a conclusion he did not intend even though he intended each individual step in the overall debacle. How could he be helped?

The likely tack of the chess-master, seeking to instruct the novice in order to save him from such failures, would very likely be to 'resolve' the game as it had been played into its component moves. In this way, the novice may reach an understanding of the contextual circumstances that led him astray through the unintended consequences of his original moves. By understanding these consequences, which he had not perceived at the time although he theoretically and potentially was capable of doing so, he realizes where he went wrong and, with the master's help, can imaginatively recompose a game plan which would avoid a repetition of the original disaster. The recomposed game, then, would not be the same as the game which was the original subject for instructive analysis.

This image of the chess-master captures very nicely Hobbes's conception of his peculiar role in relation to those he wishes to instruct in the precepts of civil philosophy. Men are like

chess novices, who blunder into political disaster because
they 'know not the causes neither of war nor peace.' And the
reason for this deficiency is that 'none hitherto have taught
them in a clear and exact method.'[60] It is this method, of
course, which Hobbes feels that he can supply and, moreover,
has put to use. The method of reckoning causes and consequences through a process of resolution and composition—
Aristotelian demonstrative science brought to practical fruition
by its adaptation to the realities of an open universe of bodies in
motion—can, in Hobbes's view, provide man with a key tool
previously unavailable in his desperate quest to solve his
political predicament. And Hobbes perceives himself as the
chief purveyor of this epistemological epiphany, a master of
the method which can save men from the horror of political
chaos.

Methodology, in other words, plays a central function in
Hobbes's political soteriology. Nature places man into a
predicament from which he must be saved—a disordered
state of nature whose perpetuation leads to mutual destruction.
To escape the likelihood of meeting a violent death, then, to
escape a 'solitary, poor, nasty, brutish, and short' existence,
man must extricate himself from the chaos of 'meer nature'
by his own effort. He may succeed in this endeavor, for he has
the capability to create social artifices, works of human craft to
make good the vacuum of order in nature. To be successful,
however, he must know his material: the natural passions, the
causes, the consequences out of which his social construct
must be created. This knowledge crucial to salvation is what
Hobbes feels he has supplied. His science of 'bodies politique'
is a redemptive tool.

On the sure foundation of the principles which Hobbes has
laid down, mankind, as the artificer by default of his own
political salvation, may build a 'constitution everlasting.'

And as the art of well building, is derived from Principles
of Reason, observed by industrious men, that had long

studied the nature of materials, and the divers effects of
figure, and proportion, long after mankind began (though
poorly) to build: So, long time after men have begun to
constitute Common-wealths, imperfect, and apt to relapse
into disorder, there may, Principles of Reason be found
out, by industrious meditation, to make their constitution
(excepting by externall violence) everlasting. And such are
those which I have in this discourse set forth.[61]

When he considers how far removed is the general practice of
men from the precepts he has discovered, Hobbes confesses,
he despairs that 'this my labour' is 'uselesse.' But as he considers again that he is the first philosopher ever to 'sufficiently
or probably prove all the Theoremes of Morall doctrine,
that man may learn thereby, both how to govern, and how to
obey,' his hopes revive. 'I recover some hope, that one time or
other, this writing of mine, may fall into the hands of a
Soveraign, who will consider it himselfe (for it is short, and I
think clear,) without the help of any interested [*sic*], or
envious Interpreter; and by the exercise of entire Soveraignty,
in protecting the Publique teaching of it, convert this Truth of
Speculation, into the Utility of Practice.'[62]

Hobbes's confidence in the efficacy of his civil philosophy as a
remedy for political disorder reflects the new status he accords
to the scientific study of politics. That is, for Hobbes, unlike for
Aristotle, political science is a theoretical science—a form of
knowledge which can be precise because it deals with necessary
truths. Hobbes, in fact, has no category of practical science;
there is only science, which is all theoretical, and untheoretized
experience. However, theoretical science, as Hobbes describes
it, takes on one very important feature of Aristotelian practical
science, namely, its orientation toward action. For Hobbes, if
the satisfactions of theoretical science were purely intrinsic
and contemplative, the game would not be worth the effort.
'For the inward glory and triumph of mind that a man may
have for the mastering of some difficult and doubtful matter, or

for the discovery of some hidden truth, is not worth so much pains as the study of Philosophy requires.'[63] Instead, knowledge must have a payoff, a concrete use or impact in our daily lives. 'The end of knowledge,' says Hobbes, echoing Bacon, 'is power'; and 'the end or scope of philosophy is, that we may make use to our benefit of effects formerly seen.'[64]

Political science, civil philosophy, is, in fact, the preeminent example of the potential practical benefits of theoretical understanding. The benefit it offers to mankind, if they will only pay heed, is nothing less than political salvation, escape from the political predicament produced by 'meer nature.' In this sense, the newly theoretical science of politics is envisaged by Hobbes as the *gnosis* of his secular and this-worldly soteriology. With this knowledge, man can save himself from political disaster. Indeed, he will inevitably save himself; for once in possession of this saving knowledge, his own nature will compel him to pursue the course of action which Hobbes prescribes. 'All men,' Hobbes asserts, 'as soon as they arrive to under-standing of this hateful condition, do desire, *even nature itself compelling them*, to be freed from this misery.'[65] Without the saving knowledge offered by the theoretical study of politic bodies, however, man cannot reckon the consequences to himself of his actions and therefore will be doomed perpetually to repeat the errors which lead to civil strife, turmoil, and warfare.

If the method which Hobbes describes and the knowledge it produces are a redemptive tool, however, they are only that. They are a necessary component of the solution to man's political predicament, but they are not by themselves sufficient for redemption. They are a tool, that is, but not a force: a vehicle, but not an impetus. They provide the necessary means which have hitherto been lacking, but in themselves they do not provide the equally necessary motivation to appropriate those means. Knowledge may be power, but it is a power contingent upon man's desire to use it. In order to discover what this force is that will, in Hobbes's view, galvanize mankind to use his doctrine if they only can understand it, we must turn to the passions of man—the other half of his nature. It is here that we must seek answers to the questions: why does man, the political (chess) novice, blunder so badly in the first place? and why will he succeed in salvaging himself once he is properly instructed in the causes and consequences of his actsion?

NOTES

1. *Leviathan*, p. 3.
2. Ibid., p. 339.
3. See for example *Metaphysics*, 1. 9. 990b ff.
4. Hobbes, *English Works*, 4: xiii.
5. 'Necessity of nature maketh men to will and desire *bonum sibi*, that which is good for themselves.' *English Works*, 4: 83.
6. Marjorie Grene, *A Portrait of Aristotle* (London: Faber and Faber Ltd., 1963), p. 87.
7. The documentation for this rather sketchy account of the basic contours of Aristotle's scientific epistemology will be found principally in the *Posterior Analytics*, which represents the keystone of his treatment of scientific method.
8. Marjorie Grene, *A Portrait of Aristotle*, p. 71.
9. As Raphael Demos has observed, Aristotle's demonstrative science is bounded in three ways: by fixed premises, by a finite number of middle terms, and by precise and definite conclusions. Science may not be expanded beyond these limits, because they represent the real limits of a finite cosmos. See 'The Structure of Substance According to Aristotle,' *Philosophy and Phenomenological Research* 5 (1944): 255–68. Cited by Grene, *A Portrait of Aristotle*.
10. For a good account of some of the apparent inconsistencies in Hobbes's epistemology, see J. W. N. Watkins, *Hobbes's System of Ideas* (London: Hutchinson University Library, 1965), esp. chapter VIII.

11. Hobbes, *English Works*, 1 : 3.

12. Aristotle, *Posterior Analytics*, 1. 2. 71b.

13. *English Works*, 2: vi.

14. He concludes there that 'circular demonstration is clearly not possible in the unqualified sense of demonstration.' *Posterior Analytics*, 1. 3. 72b.

15. *Posterior Analytics*, 1. 2. 72a.

16. *Leviathan*, p. 27.

17. *Posterior Analytics*, 1. 2. 71b. Hobbes, it may be noted, also carries over the Aristotelian requirement in the above passage that the conclusion must relate to the premises of demonstration 'as effect to cause.' He writes: 'The end of science is the demonstration of the causes and generations of things; which if they be not in the definitions, they cannot be found in the conclusion of the first syllogism, that is made from those definitions; and if they be not in the first conclusion, they will not be found in any further conclusion deduced from that; and, therefore, by proceeding in this manner, we shall never come to science; which is against the scope and intention of demonstration.' (*English Works*, 1 : 82–83.)

18. *Posterior Analytics*, 1. 3. 72b.

19. *English Works*, 1 : 80.

20. *Posterior Analytics*, 2. 3. 90b.

21. *English Works*, 1 : 37.

22. *English Works*, 1 : 81.

23. *English Works*, 2 : 305.

24. Grene, *A Portrait of Aristotle*, p. 87.

25. To cite Grene's excellent study again: Aristotle found that 'things in the natural world present themselves to our minds, whose nature it is to be receiving such presentation, as *definable*.' Grene observes, 'I need not stress here again that this discovery, while the moralist's despair, is the biologist's daily stock in trade' (p. 85).

26. *Posterior Analytics*, 2. 3. 90b.

27. *De Corpore*, 1 : 21, 56, 60.

28. 'Whensoever that thing has a name, the definition of it can

be nothing but the explication of that name by speech.'
(*English Works*, 1: 83.)

29. *English Works*, 1: 83–84.

30. Ibid., pp. 16 and 37. For a good treatment of the nature
and complexities of Hobbes's nominalism, see J. W. N.
Watkins, *Hobbes's System of Ideas*, Chapt. 8.

31. 'In the right Definition of Names, lyes the first use of
Speech; which is the Acquisition of Science.' (*Leviathan*, p. 27.)

32. *English Works*, 1: 83.

33. Although Hobbes specifies recurrent forms of definitional
'incoherencies' which are, to his view, the principal sources
of philosophical error (see *English Works*, 1, Chapt. 5, entitled 'Of Erring, Falsity, and Captions'), there are great
gaps yet to be filled. For example, nowhere does he (or can he)
specify formal criteria for adjudicating whether his proffered
definition of justice ('For all these words, Hee that in his
actions observeth the Lawes of his Country, make but one
Name, equivalent to this one word, Just,' *Leviathan*, p. 24.) is
right and a conflicting definition (e.g., a just man is one who
always follows his conscience) false.

34. Cf. English Works, 2: 305; 1: 388; 7: 222; and *Leviathan*,
p. 27.

35. *Posterior Analytics*, 2. 19. 100a.

36. *English Works*, 1: 66.

37. Ibid., p. 389; see also p. 399.

38. Ibid., 1: 27.

39. *Posterior Analytics*, 2. 19. 100b.

40. *Topics*, 1. 1. 100b. For further elaboration of the indispensable role of reliable intuition in Aristotelian epistemology,
see Grene, *A Portrait of Aristotle*, pp. 109–12.

41. *English Works*, 1: 84. See also ibid., p. 81: 'And names of
the former kind are well enough defined, when, by speech as
short as may be, we raise in the mind of the hearer perfect
and clear ideas or conceptions of the things named.'

42. Speaking of *nous*, Herbert Marcuse observes: 'Indeed this
evidence of intuition is not too different from the Cartesian

one.' *One-Dimensional Man* (Boston: Beacon Press, 1964), p. 126.

43. *English Works*, 1: 66.

44. 'By ratiocination, I mean computation.' *English Works*, 1: 3.

45. *English Works*, 1: 10. Hobbes can therefore equate science and mathematics: 'Science, namely the Mathematiques . . .' *Leviathan*, p. 70.

46. *Leviathan*, p. 32.

47. See Aristotle, *Posterior Analytics*, 1. 2. 72a, and Hobbes, *English Works*, 1: 66–67.

48. *Posterior Analytics*, 2. 19. 100b.

49. *English Works*, 1: 68–69. Having resolved singular things into 'such things as are most universal,' then, Hobbes feels that the rest is easy, since the cause of all universal things is some form of motion. 'But the causes of universal things . . . are manifest of themselves, or (as they commonly say) known to nature; so that they need no method at all; for they have all but one universal cause, which is motion.' Ibid., p. 69.

50. 'The cause and generation of such things, as have any cause or generation, ought to enter into the definitions.' Hobbes, *English Works*, 1: 82.

51. Aristotle, *Posterior Analytics*, 1. 18. 81b and 1. 24. 85b.

52. Hobbes, *English Works*, 1: 82–3.

53. Ibid., p. 81.

54. Ibid., 2: xiv.

55. Ibid., p. xvii.

56. Ibid., p. xviii.

57. This universal acquiescence to his doctrine which Hobbes sees as a possibility can result: first, because his logic will command the assent of reason by logical compulsion; and second, because his principles will command the assent of the passions by natural compulsion. 'They who have written of justice and policy in general, do all invade each other and themselves with contradictions. To reduce this doctrine to the rules and infallibility of reason, there is no way, but, first, put such principles down for a foundation, as passion, not mis-

trusting, may not seek to displace; and afterwards to build thereon the truth of cases in the law of nature (which hitherto have been built in the air) by degrees, till the whole have been inexpungable.' *English Works*, 4, Epistle dedicatory.

58. *English Works*, 1: 8. (Emphasis added.)
59. J. W. N. Watkins, *Hobbes's System of Ideas*, pp. 78–79.
60. *English Works*, 1: 8.
61. *Leviathan*, p. 290.
62. Ibid., pp. 318–19.
63. *English Works*, 1: 7.
64. Ibid.
65. Ibid., 2: xvii. (Emphasis added.)

6

Passion and the Politics of Containment

'It is evident that the polis belongs to the class of
things that exist by nature, and that man is by nature
an animal intended to live in a polis.' — *Aristotle.*

'And thus much for the ill condition, which man by
meer nature is actually placed in, though with a
possibility to come out of it.' — *Hobbes.*

The two principal components of man's nature are his cognitive
capacities and his affective inclinations. In the previous chapter
the nature and significance of Hobbes's conception of human
reason, its powers and processes, were discussed. His basic view
of man's rationality, it was argued, is an adaptation of the
Aristotelian epistemological format to the exigencies of the
seventeenth-century's new view of reality. Moreover, it was
noted, Hobbes is convinced that reason, so conceived, has a
critical role in the deliverance of man from his political plight.
To complete the sketch of Hobbes's view of human nature, it
is necessary now to consider his treatment of human passion
and its political consequences.

It is here, in the realm of human passion, that Hobbes finds
the dynamic forces behind the political struggle. The drama of
political life for him is the product of the interplay between
contending fundamental motivations which govern the actions
of all men. These motivations are universal, natural drives, in
his view, as much an essential part of man as the natural facts
of his corporeality and mortality.

The political impact of the natural framework of human passions is, for Hobbes, profoundly paradoxical. Man's emotional

necessities are both his blessing and his curse, the source of his immediate quandary and his potential deliverance. For on the one hand, man's natural egoism propels him into a primal political imbroglio of zero-sum game competition with his fellow human beings. The satisfaction of his egoistic desires logically requires the frustration of other men's desires. It is for this reason that the natural condition of mankind is seen as a state of war. On the other hand, man's natural desire to avoid violent death constitutes a great pacifier. Man is never really socialized, for Hobbes, in the sense of deriving great reciprocal satisfaction from social interaction, but he may be socialized to the limited extent of providing for the containment of his destructive egoism. And the motivating force behind this politics of containment is part of man's natural passion as surely as are the forces which create his political dilemma in the first place.

The bearing of Hobbes's basic cosmology, his view of motion, body, and nature, upon his psychology and politics is a controversial issue. Some writers have accepted Hobbes's belief that his political and psychological ideas were firmly based upon his natural philosophy. Hobbes's contemporaries, especially, were inclined to see his materialism, his alleged atheism, and his politics as all part of one detestable whole. Since G. C. Robertson argued that Hobbes's political ideas were largely formulated when he was still simply an observer of men and manners rather than a natural philosopher, however, there has been a strong tendency to separate his social thought from his cosmological ideas. Robertson found the key sources of Hobbes's political theory in 'his personal circumstances and the events of his time'; Strauss found these sources in Hobbes's conception of natural right; and Taylor and Warrender found these sources in Hobbes's allegedly autonomous belief in the existence of natural or divine obligations.[1] Despite the differences among themselves, these writers share the view that the basic source of Hobbes's political thought is not to be found in his natural philosophy.

The logic behind Strauss's dismissal of Hobbes's natural philosophy as a genuine basis of his political philosophy is significant. Earlier metaphysics were, he says, 'anthropomorphistic' and 'therefore a proper basis for the philosophy of things human.' On the other hand, modern science 'which tried to interpret nature by renouncing all anthropomorphisms, all conceptions of purpose and perfection, could, therefore, to say the least, contribute nothing to the understanding of things human, to the foundation of morals and politics.'[2] Hobbes's 'original view,' Strauss concludes, 'is independent both of tradition and modern science.'[3]

J. W. N. Watkins aptly summarizes the Strauss–Warrender–Taylor–Robertson position this way: 'Psychological conclusions about thoughts, feelings, and wants cannot be deduced from materialistic premises about body movements; therefore Hobbes must have made a fresh start when he turned from nature to psychology and politics.'[4] The major premise of this argument is, I think, beyond serious disputation. Structural features of one realm of reality cannot be derived by deducing them from the characteristic features of another realm. Psychological and political principles cannot be deduced from physiological principles. Nevertheless, the conclusion of the argument—'therefore Hobbes must have made a fresh start'— is not easily reconcilable with Hobbes's own conception of what he was doing, nor does it necessarily follow from the major premise. The problem is that there is a hidden minor premise in the 'fresh start' argument, namely, that the only form of influence of natural philosophy on political philosophy is by direct substantive, deductive, influence. This premise, however, is based upon an overly narrow conception of the operations of the human mind. And if this minor premise is denied, then the conclusion that Hobbes must have made a fresh start when he turned to politics and psychology can also be denied.

Contrary to the hidden minor premise in the 'fresh start' theory, there is more than one way in which a theoretical formulation in one area may exert some influence over theoretical formulations in another area. Or, to express it in the concrete terms of the immediate problem, there is more than one way in which the transformation of the idea of nature in the seventeenth century, which Hobbes embraces, could have had a positive impact upon his political theory. In certain cases one area of theory may conceivably have direct, substantive implications for another area of theory. If political life is a part of the larger whole of natural life, then a change in the substantive understanding of nature will obviously have a direct, deductive bearing upon the understanding of politics. The substantive properties of the part are transformed with the substantive properties of the whole. In the case of Hobbes, however, this mode of influence is not really a logical possibility, since as Strauss has pointed out, his conception of nature has no human substantive properties at all.

Hobbes, considering man to be part of nature, may have entertained the idea that his political theory could be derived deductively from his natural philosophy. If he did entertain this view, he was mistaken for the reasons Strauss puts forward. However, his conviction that his natural philosophy had a profound impact upon his political outlook was not mistaken, even if he misconstrued how the impact came about.

Even where one theoretical model cannot properly produce a theoretical model appropriate to another realm of reality by a process of logical deduction, it may have a profound influence upon the other area of theory by means of analogy. Theory developed to explain one area of reality — the motion of physical bodies, for example — may have a persuasive structuring impact upon a second theoretical model directed toward understanding another area of reality — the emotions of human beings, for example. The formulations of one theory do not govern the other theory in a direct, deductive way; they have their impact by analogically shaping the perceptual patterns used to relate and tie together the raw data of the area in question. Models and metaphors which were developed to conceptualize one set of data, especially if they are seen as properly relevant to another set of data, may serve to establish the conceptual patterns which are used to understand that other set of data.

While it is true that Hobbes's natural philosophy cannot provide the content of his political theory, then, it serves as a source of heuristic models which shape and limit his political theory analogically. 'Nature' for Hobbes is devoid not only of human substance but of any substance other than that homogeneous substance which he calls 'body.' Nature, however, does have a characteristic pattern of action. It moves in a specific, definable fashion, the apprehension of which is 'the gateway of natural philosophy universal.' And it is this model of behavior which Hobbes carries over by analogy into his explication of human political and psychological behavior.

The extension of this model of behavior from the realm of natural philosophy to the realm of political philosophy was not merely a possible theoretical assumption which Hobbes happened to make. He was instead positively led to take this step by the framework of the Aristotelian cosmology which he tacitly accepted as the proper matrix of his own world view. For although the Aristotelian–Scholastic cosmos was composed of heterogeneous substances, it was depicted as quite homogeneous in its basic pattern of action. Specifically, the Aristotelian model depicted all natural motion as manifesting the same basic pattern of the actualization of potentiality. Men, plants, animals, and falling bodies all allegedly exhibited the universal properties of natural motion—they all were striving to reach their natural *telos*.

In other words, it was one of the implicit propositions of the Aristotelian cosmology that everything that moved naturally moved in the same way. There were no discontinuities among varied types of natural motion, no lines of differentiation among different characteristic modes of behaving in different forms of life. Therefore, it was a natural assumption for Hobbes to make that the transformed conception of motion possessed universal applicability. Against the background of the intellectual tradition in which he had been trained, it would have been a revolutionary step for him to have thought otherwise. Since his philosophic radicalism extended only to a drastic metamorphosis of the Aristotelian cosmology, and not to its outright abandonment, it was easy for him to presume that human behavior should be perceived and interpreted in fundamentally the same manner as the behavior of other constituents of nature. Aristotle in effect invited this presumption, and Hobbes acquiesced. Substantively radical, he remains formally conservative.

Paradoxically, in fact, Hobbes's retention of the matrix of the Aristotelian cosmology contributes importantly to the totality of his substantive rejection of Aristotelian doctrines. Since the formal pattern of the Aristotelian cosmology established the profound interconnectedness of all the substances of nature by using a single theoretical conception of motion as their common foundation, it invited its own wholesale destruction. By resting his entire cosmology upon the foundation of a single theoretical model, Aristotle constructed a world view that was as fragile as it was extensive. In effect, anyone who could legitimately transform the theoretical foundation of his cosmology — his idea of motion — could transform the entire edifice. Hobbes, in effect, did precisely that.

The relationship of Hobbes's new model of motion and the natural philosophy which develops from it to his political and psychological theories is not a simple one. Past discussions of the problem have tended to miscarry by assuming that Hobbes's natural philosophy either produces his political theory in its entirety or else it is irrelevant. The choices, however, need not be constrained by this dichotomy. In fact, Hobbes's natural philosophy is neither the sufficient basis of his political theory nor irrelevant. It has profound bearing without constituting sufficient cause.

Since, as Strauss observed, there is no human content in the new cosmology it simply cannot be the source of a substantive political theory. No amount of intellectual contortioning can remedy that fundamental incapacity. The new philosophy of nature, however, did inculcate in its adherents, Hobbes among them, a faith in the efficacy of certain organizational paradigms as interpreters of reality. If these perceptual patterns, or paradigms, could be made legitimately applicable to human phenomena—and the Aristotelian cosmology suggested the legitimacy of such a carry-over—then they might become profoundly significant in shaping and ordering this set of data as well. Considerable evidence suggests that this potential form of influence of natural philosophy upon social philosophy is in fact operative in Hobbes.

In order for perceptual models of natural philosophy to become influential in shaping perceptions of political order, it is necessary for them to achieve what might be called *resonance* with some patterns found in the realm of politics. That is, the theorist must perceive, or believe he perceives, political realities which are relatively isomorphic with the model which has developed from a consideration of natural realities. Apart from a situation of this sort, paradigms derived from the interpretation of the natural world will have little or no bearing upon the interpretation of politics. If there is a predisposition to see paradigms of nature as relevant to politics, and if in addition these paradigms can achieve some resonance with significant political phenomena, then a philosophy of nature may have a real impact on a theory of politics.

In the case of Hobbes, as I shall argue, the determinative models in his interpretation of nature do have resonance in some fundamental components of politics—especially in the area of human passion and motivation. In human vanity, egocentricity, appetiveness, desire for power, and self-preservation, Hobbes found aspects of human behavior which lent themselves readily in his view to conceptualization by the same basic models that had proved so fruitful in the understanding of natural phenomena. Moreover, he was conditioned by Aristotelianism to view these parallelisms as more than interesting analogies, to see them instead as manifestations of the fundamental homogeneity of all 'natural action,' human behavior included.

Since paradigms originating in extrapolitical, nonhuman areas of investigation must achieve resonance in political reality, it could be argued that they are not especially potent in political theory. Perhaps they serve as merely illustrative analogies which are used for purposes of communication or elaboration. Perhaps they are largely rhetorical window dressing that could be jettisoned without altering the theory notably.

It is possible to construct a plausible argument along these lines. And such an argument can never be definitively adjudicated, since it rests upon conjecture as to 'what would otherwise have been the case.' Any answer given, therefore, is subject to the same kinds of reservations as answers to conjectural historical puzzles, such as 'what would have happened had the South won the Civil War?' and 'what would Europe be like now if the Bolshevik Revolution had been a failure?' The contribution of natural science paradigms to political theories, therefore, can never be precisely measured. However, it is necessary and important to observe that these paradigms can perform several functions in the context of political theory which go considerably beyond a merely decorative or rhetorical role. When these functions are noted, it becomes a persuasive supposition that the political theories in question would not be the same in the absence of the suggestive paradigms, nor would they be as strongly held and widely applied. At the very least, the presence of these positive functions of the extrapolitically originated paradigms in the context of political theory shifts the burden of proof to those who would argue that they are not significantly influential even where clearly present.

In the first place, paradigms which originate from the interpretation of nonpolitical phenomena may play a part in the actual process of formation of a political theory. By establishing a given pattern of order in the mind of the theorist, a nonpolitical model may suggest to him basic structures and forms which he could use to understand politics. It may serve, in other words, as a kind of catalytic agent which helps to consolidate and integrate the political data into gestalts which have already proved persuasive in other contexts. The human mind is not divided into separate compartments. When a person turns from one set of data to another, from one type of intellectual problem to another, he cannot simultaneously purge his mind of all the patterns and concepts he has perceived and used. Even if he were to approach every new realm of reality only after undergoing a Cartesian mental purgative — and Hobbes by no means felt this to be necessary or even appropriate methodologically — he could not escape the influence of his conceptual predispositions established by previous experience. Therefore, it is more than merely possible that a paradigm which is itself nonpolitical in origin may play a profound role in the formation of political concepts. And since Hobbes, beginning with the assumption of the homogeneity of 'natural motion' which he took over from the Aristotelian tradition, conceives this kind of conceptual carry-over to be perfectly proper if not positively imperative, this possibility becomes a likelihood in his particular case.

It is difficult if not impossible to demonstrate conclusively the formative influence of an established paradigm on the creation of another theoretical model. This difficulty arises because the operations of the human mind in the process of scientific discovery (as contrasted with the application and verification of theory) are extremely obscure. Ever since Plato posed the problem in the *Meno*, it has remained a mystery, both in philosophy and in science, precisely how the mind goes about looking for something which it does not know.[5] What we do know about these intellectual processes of discovery, however, based upon the reports of creative scientists who have made significant discoveries, suggests that paradigms, models, images, gestalts stemming from a wide variety of sources unrelated to the immediate subject-matter may play a profound role in the germination of theories. The chemist who discovered the circular structure of a particular hydrocarbon molecule, for example, reported that the catalyst to his discovery was a dream in which he saw a snake holding its tail in its mouth. Surely, then, it is not too difficult to perceive that a dramatic new paradigm which had clearly possessed the mind of a given theorist, as the model of inertial motion had done in the case of Hobbes, might perform a similar function of creative inspiration through the medium of persuasive analogy.

If the extrapolitical paradigm which is used in the interpretation of politics has its origin in the very fundamental realm of nature, it serves a second positive function in relation to the political theory. It serves to give cosmological status to the political theory. It gives to the theory an alleged foundation that it does not possess in and of itself and therefore enhances its standing. An interpretation of politics carries an added claim to allegiance if it can be presented as but one manifestation of a much broader, indeed universal, force or tendency which is present in the very foundation of the universe. For example, the pattern of economic behavior captured by the law of supply and demand constitutes a significant analytical perception in its own right; but it achieves even more clout when it is presented as a law of nature that shares a common grounding with other natural patterns of orderliness.

This function of providing a cosmological foundation for a social theory was especially significant in the period following the scientific revolution for at least two reasons. In the first place, such an alleged relationship between natural order and political order replicated the traditional pattern of finding nature to be a significant agent in the shaping of political realities. Although the substantive content of both the new view of nature and the new political theories of the seventeenth century and the Enlightenment were quite different from the content of the traditional view of nature and of politics, the ostensive functional relationship between the two was maintained by connecting them through a common paradigm. And second, the age following the scientific revolution has been one in which the tools and models used to understand the world of nature have achieved a unique preeminence. The surest path to legitimating virtually any form of inquiry has been to appropriate or approximate the methods of the mathematicizing sciences.[6] As a consequence, the claim that a particular social theory was firmly grounded scientifically —i.e., on the foundation of natural philosophy—improved its credibility not only to the theorist's audience but also to the theorist himself.

In this context, then, Hobbes had considerable cause to shape his political perceptions and formulations so that they would conform fairly closely to the theoretical patterns of his natural philosophy. Significant benefits accrued to his system to the extent that he shaped and tailored one part of it to be symmetrical with the rest. The coherence of the whole constituted a powerful argument on behalf of each of its parts. Moreover, these compelling forces at work on behalf of integration and isomorphism among the varied parts of Hobbes's system of ideas should not be viewed as a purely external force. That is, he was not encouraged to dovetail his natural and political philosophies merely for the sake of persuading others; he was encouraged to do so to satisfy criteria of proper theoretical form profoundly operative within his own mind. He was himself sincerely convinced that the permeation of political concepts by the paradigms of natural philosophy was not only proper, but compulsory. He genuinely felt that civil philosophy 'cannot be demonstrated, till [natural philosophy] be fully understood.'[7]

Once a paradigm growing from natural philosophy has become firmly established and then legitimated as appropriately adaptable to political theorizing, moreover, it influences the resultant political theory in yet another way. Besides performing a catalytic function in the formation of the theoretical model and serving to give it cosmological status, the reliance upon a paradigm serves to stabilize and to reinforce the theory that has been generated and legitimated. This function of stabilization and reinforcement proceeds in both a positive and a negative fashion.

Negatively, the model taken as a legitimate paradigm serves as a principle of conceptual limitation. The lines of the paradigm, in other words, not only legitimate what lies within them but also exclude what falls beyond them. Phenomena which do not correspond to the established pattern, which transcend the boundaries of the paradigm, may easily remain unnoticed. These phenomena may be rendered virtually invisible, since the established perceptual gestalt refines them out rather like a polarized lens. Or, alternatively, their presence may be explicitly denied since they cannot conform with, cannot fit into, the accepted perceptual mold. Michael Polanyi has termed this limiting function of an accepted model the 'principle of suppressed nucleation.' That is, the model functions to 'deny to any rival conception the ground in which it might take root. Experiences which support it could be adduced only one by one. But a new conception . . . could be established only by a whole series of relevant instances, and such evidence cannot accumulate in the minds of people if each of them is disregarded in its turn for lack of the concept which would lend significance to it.'[8] The conception of nature which Hobbes brings with him to the study of politics exerts some of its most profound influence, I shall argue below, in this manner. On the basis of his preestablished model of the world, some significant realities and possibilities are denied, jettisoned, or not seriously considered because their accreditation would break the boundaries of the model.

Positively, i.e., beyond this negative function of limitation, the use of such an established conceptual model serves to reinforce and stabilize the theories it generates by a process of heuristic expansion. Once the model has been certified as the representation of a universal pattern of order, it tends to shape perceptions of other phenomena in such a way as to integrate them into its framework. A paradigm which has ostensive universal status, which allegedly characterizes the universal nature of things, will possess this kind of expansibility almost by logical implication. If this is the very model of nature, the logic runs, then surely it is capable of expanding its explanatory scope to encompass any product of nature, including the state of nature.

To summarize the argument to this point, then, it is quite possible for a philosophy of nature to exert a considerable impact on a philosophy of things human, even if that philosophy of nature is not anthropomorphic. By offering basic models which are held to be paradigmatic of the created world as a whole, even a nonanthropomorphic natural philosophy may work by analogy to shape, to suggest, to limit, to consolidate, to expand, to substantiate, to stabilize, and to reinforce formally parallel models of political life. In what follows I shall argue that in Hobbes's system of ideas this possible mode of influence is in fact operative and influential.

It is not possible, of course, to demonstrate beyond question that Hobbes's political thought is influenced in the ways specified above by his natural philosophy. The only possible proof of this would be his own statements not only asserting that this is the case but explaining how it is the case. And even then one might argue, as in effect Leo Strauss did, that there is no real influence of this sort operative and that insofar as Hobbes thought there was he was simply mistaken.[9] What may be demonstrated, however, are the following: 1) Hobbes thought that natural philosophy should be the foundation of political theory; 2) Hobbes thought that he had in fact succeeded in grounding his political theory on such a foundation; 3) some very striking parallels are present between the conceptual forms fundamental to Hobbes's view of nature and conceptual forms centrally operative in his depiction of political order; 4) certain possibilities and realities which might be perceived in politics (some of which in fact played an important role in the traditional view of politics) are rejected by Hobbes, and such a rejection would be a logical consequence of accepting as definitive of political behavior models of behavior originating in his natural philosophy.

The first two of these propositions have been largely established by this time, and in any case they are not very controversial. We shall turn then to an elaboration and substantiation of the latter two propositions, examining the significant gestalts and exclusions in Hobbes's political theory which run parallel to similar patterns and limitations in his view of nature. Taken together these claims do not substantiate any belief that Hobbes's political theory is purely derivative of his natural philosophy; and such, indeed, is not in fact the case. What they do add up to is a warrant for belief that Hobbes's political ideas were significantly shaped and limited by the conjunction of his substantive natural philosophy and his methodological belief that natural and political philosophy were properly interrelated.

The motif in Hobbes's view of nature which has the most profound and pervasive carry-over into his psychological and political models is his conception of motion. Tacitly standing within the formal matrix of his eviscerated Aristotelian cosmology, Hobbes assumes that the entire natural order including man, 'that most excellent work of Nature,' moves in fundamentally the same way. What Hobbes sees to be this basically homogeneous pattern of motion, however, has been radically recast. The universal phenomenon of motion is depicted by Hobbes as revealed by the startlingly new and fruitful theory of inertia.

The Aristotelian mind had looked at all the hustle and bustle of the world, all the 'natural' motion constantly going on, and had seen it as the pursuit of finite ends by the phenomena of nature. The world's action was the interplay of purposeful strivings toward rest and fulfillment. Having incorporated the conceptual transformation manifested by the new understanding of inertia, Hobbes looked upon the world and saw the interplay of motions with no natural end, no place of 'rest' whatsoever. 'Rest' was purely a relative situation, and it came

about in a moving body only through the imposition of an
external force. This way of perceiving motion is not restricted
by Hobbes to a single stratum of reality; it is seen as applicable
to the motions of human and political bodies as well as to the
motions of physical bodies. Therefore, Hobbes, early in
Leviathan, establishes the model of inertia as a valid paradigm
for the interpretation of moving bodies: 'That when a thing lies
still, unlesse somewhat els stirre it, it will lye still for ever, is a
truth that no man doubts of. But that when a thing is in motion,
it will eternally be in motion, unless somewhat els stay it,
though the reason be the same, (namely, that nothing can
change itselfe,) is not so easily assented to.'[10]

The analogical carry-over into the interpretation of human,
political phenomena of the new motion model leads Hobbes to a
profoundly significant assumption from which his political
theory must begin: men, too, move inertially. Not physical
motions alone, but human e-motions as well move end-lessly,
restlessly. Human motives are not specific finite desires which
may be terminated by their fulfillment. Human life is not the
quest of definite ends whose attainment brings the quest to a
satisfied conclusion. Instead, as motivationally inertial creatures,
like all the world, men move endlessly and insatiably. Therefore
Hobbes postulates 'for a generall inclination of all mankind,
a perpetuall and restless desire of Power after power, that
ceaseth only in death.'[11] His fundamental psychological model,
that is, is a human equivalent of the law of inertia. Elsewhere
he elaborates: 'Seeing all delight is appetite, and presupposeth
a further end, there can be no contentment but in proceeding:
and therefore we are not to marvel, when we see, that as men
attain to more riches, honour, or other power; so their appetite
continually groweth more and more; and when they are come
to the utmost degree of some kind of power, they pursue some
other, as long as in any kind they think themselves behind
any other.'[12]

In the Aristotelian cosmos, everything was characterized by a
tendency to self-fulfillment. Movement was essentially a form

M

of growth or development. And man's movements, his
e-motions, were one species of this universal pattern. His
desire (*orexis*) and his natural tendency (*hormē*) were directed
toward finite ends which terminated the desire and the motion
it engendered by fulfilling it. In Hobbes's world of inertial
motion, this fundamental metaphysical postulate is transformed from the perception of a universal tendency of all things
natural to grow into a belief that all nature possesses a universal
tendency to persist. All nature fundamentally desires its self-
preservation; it wishes, inertially, to persevere in its established
path. Man, as a natural creature, is no different. He is possessed
by an overriding natural tendency to seek his self-preservation.
This desire, as a universal tendency of nature, is not properly
subject to praise or blame, any more than one could be blamed
for having two arms and a head. Not to have this desire would
be perverse, unnatural. 'For every man is desirous of what is
good for him, and shuns what is evil, but chiefly the chiefest of
natural evils, which is death; and this he doth by a certain
impulsion of nature, no less than that whereby a stone moves
downward. It is therefore neither absurd nor reprehensible,
neither against the dictates of true reason, for a man to use all
his endeavours to preserve and defend his body and the members thereof from death and sorrows.'[13]

This fundamental, irreducible natural desire to persist in
one's being, to preserve oneself, Hobbes continues, is the
ontological foundation of natural right. 'Therefore, the first
foundation of natural right is this, that every man as much as in
him lies endeavour to protect his life and members.'[14] While it
is true, therefore, as Strauss has insisted, that 'Hobbes's political
philosophy starts from natural right,'[15] it must be recognized
that natural right is for Hobbes simply the legitimation of the
basic overwhelming motive force of the world. Natural right is
not an *a priori* moral postulate which Hobbes promulgates as
the central premise of his political theory. It is merely the
realistic recognition and acceptance of the givenness in his
own nature which man did not create and cannot abolish.

Hobbes elaborates this connection of natural tendency and natural right in an important passage in the *Elements of Law*. That which is done by 'necessity of nature' constitutes a 'blameless liberty,' he asserts, and that is what is meant by a 'right.'

> And forasmuch as necessity of nature maketh men to will and desire *bonum sibi*, that which is good for themselves, and to avoid that which is hurtful; but most of all, the terrible enemy of nature, death, from whom we expect both the loss of all power, and also the greatest of bodily pains in the losing; it is not against reason, that a man doth all he can to preserve his own body and limbs both from death and pain. And that which is not against reason, men call *right*, or *jus*, or *blameless liberty* of using our own natural power and ability. It is therefore a right of nature, that every man may preserve his own life and limbs, with all the power he hath.[16]

This nexus between natural right and the universal natural tendency of all created things to preserve themselves is the nexus between 'is' and 'ought' in Hobbes's political theory which has been alleged since Hume to be a logical impropriety. Hobbes's defense against this charge of impropriety would, I think, be essentially as follows. 'I did not confer the status of right upon natural tendency,' he might say. 'Nature herself did that. It is natural right that is in question, after all, not legal right or my personal preference. Only madmen moralize in a vacuum; and once nature instilled in all men a given inevitable desire, it was not in my power to declare the desire illegitimate any more than one could hurl imprecations against the rising of the tides or the falling of heavy bodies. Authority confers right, and nature is the author of man's innate drive for self-preservation. Hence nature (or God, as the author of nature, if you wish) has made this a natural right, and to begin political theory at this fixed point is only an act of acquiescence in what nature has given us; it is an act of sanity and of science, not the promulgation of a moral dictate.'

It helps to substantiate the claim that Hobbes took seriously what he felt to be the implications of his natural philosophy for the understanding of psychology and politics to observe similar thought patterns in the work of his noted contemporary, Spinoza. For Spinoza had also absorbed the philosophical implications of the new cosmology; and therefore, if Hobbes's social ideas are not based purely upon his observation of men and manners, but in significant part on his natural philosophy, then his thought might well exhibit some important conceptual parallelisms with Spinoza's. And indeed, Spinoza, in his *Ethics*, articulates a position which is strikingly similar to that of Hobbes, formally, substantively, and methodologically.

The key formal and methodological parallelism between Hobbes and Spinoza consists in their belief that: 1) man is a part of the whole of nature; 2) he therefore must be approached as one would approach a natural phenomenon, not to praise or blame it, but to understand it; 3) the method for understanding man's nature is the same as the method for understanding nature in general and therefore is a kind of quasigeometry. Hobbes's assent to these propositions has already been observed. Spinoza's commitment to them appears very clearly in the third part of his *Ethics*, 'On the Origin and Nature of the Affects.' Spinoza begins by complaining that most men approach human action as though it were a special case, altogether apart from the 'common laws of nature':

Most persons who have written about the affects and man's conduct of life seem to discuss, not the natural things which follow the common laws of nature, but things which are outside her. They seem indeed to consider man in nature as a kingdom within a kingdom. For they believe that man disturbs rather than follows her order; that he has an absolute power over his own actions; and that he is altogether self-determined. They then proceed to attribute

the cause of human weakness and changeableness, not to
the common power of nature, but to some vice of human
nature, which they therefore bewail, laugh at, mock, or, as
is more generally the case, detest.[17]

In contrast to this approach, Spinoza states, he will take
quite a different tack; and this change of method is based upon
an explicit affirmation of the homogeneity of nature and
nature's product, man, just as Hobbes could have stated it:

> To such as these it will doubtless seem a marvellous thing
> for me to endeavour to treat by a geometrical method the
> vices and follies of men, and to desire by a sure method to
> demonstrate those things which these people cry out against
> as being vanities, absurdities, and monstrosities. The
> following is my reason for so doing. Nothing happens in
> nature which can be attributed to any vice of nature, for
> she is always the same and everywhere one. Her virtue is
> the same, and her power of acting; . . . so that there must
> also be one and the same method of understanding the
> nature of all things whatsoever, that is to say, by the
> universal laws and rules of nature. The affects, therefore,
> of hatred, anger, envy, considered in themselves, follow
> from the same necessity and virtue of nature as other
> individual things. . . . I shall, therefore . . . consider
> human actions and appetites just as if I were considering
> lines; planes, or bodies.[18]

The parallelism between Spinoza and Hobbes, moreover, is
not purely formal and methodological; it extends also to the
central substantive conception of the content of nature's 'power
of acting' as manifested in human life. Having established the
fundamental homogeneity of natural motion, and having found
the concept of inertia to be the paradigm of this motion,[19]
Spinoza infers that the *conatus sese conservandi*, the desire for
self-preservation, is the basic natural tendency of all life. This

principle is enunciated in Proposition Six of Part Three: 'Each thing, in so far as it is in itself, endeavours to persevere in its being.'[20] Hobbes, then, is not alone in deriving from the new cosmology the concept of an inertial drive for self-preservation as the fundamental natural tendency of human behavior.

The natural necessity impelling all men to seek their self-preservation generates the quest for power which is central to Hobbes's view of human motivation. In part, that is, the 'rest-less' search for power which men exhibit is a practical consequence of their desire to avoid meeting a violent end. Trying to prevent others from endangering him, a man in the state of nature will naturally be driven to seek mastery over them. 'There is no way for any man to secure himselfe, so reasonable, as Anticipation; that is, by force, or wiles, to master the persons of all men he can, so long, till he see no other power great enough to endanger him: And this is no more than his own conservation requireth.'[21]

The *libido dominandi*, then, arises in the first place from the necessities of self-preservation. However, the matter is not quite as simple as that. There are at least two other sources of the restless desire for power which Hobbes sees as operative in men. The first of these is the love of glory, human vanity. Some men, Hobbes says, desire dominion over others not simply for the sake of security, but because they take delight in possessing the eminence manifested in their power. 'There be some,' he says, who pursue their acts of conquest 'further then their security requires' because they 'take pleasure in contemplating their own power in the acts of conquest.'[22]

The other source of man's quest for power might be expressed this way: power is necessary to liberty which is necessary to motion which is the source of human contentment. Power is a *sine qua non* of the continuing motion which is the essence of human happiness. 'Delight, contentment, or pleasure,' Hobbes tells us, 'is nothing really but motion about the heart . . . and the objects that cause it are called pleasant or delightful.'[23] 'There can be no contentment,' he says elsewhere, 'but in proceeding.'[24] For a man to be happy, therefore, he must be capable of moving as he pleases. That is, his motion must be unimpeded or else he will be frustrated and unhappy. Happiness, then, requires liberty, since liberty is unimpeded motion. 'Liberty, or Freedome, signifieth (properly) the absence of Opposition: (by Opposition, I mean externall Impediments of motion).'[25] Because other men and their desires represent opposition to any man's natural desires, however, it becomes necessary to his liberty that he have power; for it is power alone that permits him to overcome the opposition and continue in his desired path. Therefore, it is a natural conjunction when Hobbes writes that men 'naturally love Liberty, and Dominion over others.'[26] The latter is a necessary means to the former.

To summarize, then, the fundamental paradigm of inertia as the pattern of 'natural action' has a profound shaping influence upon the basic motivational psychology from which Hobbes begins his consideration of the nature and tasks of political order. In the first place, the conceptualization of the *libido dominandi* is isomorphic with the conceptual pattern of inertia: the search for power is 'perpetuall and restlesse,' having no end short of death.[27] And second, the inertial model of human motivation provides two of the three sources in Hobbes's genetic account of the centrality of the quest for power in human life: inertia in the form of the *conatus sese conservandi*, and inertia as 'delight in proceeding.' The third is delight in contemplating one's own preeminence, that is, glory. This third source of the power drive is not derived from models suggested by Hobbes's natural philosophy, but simply from his observations about human nature. He integrated it into his basic model of human behavior, but it is in origin philosophically autonomous, a product of, as G. C. Robertson put it, his 'observations of men and manners.'[28]

Moreover, the conception of a natural tendency to persevere in motion as a universal attribute of all natural beings, including man, is the ontological basis of Hobbes's concept of natural right. Therefore, the new view of motion, the critical fulcrum of Hobbes's 'natural philosophy universal' permeates his political thought in the roles of: 1) the formal pattern of his political psychology, 2) a dynamic source of his derivation of the *libido dominandi*, and 3) the 'empirical' foundation of his formulation of natural right. Although his nonanthropomorphic natural philosophy could not provide the concrete human substance for his political and psychological theory, therefore (as the ambiguous role of glory in his thought illustrates), his political theory hardly represents a fresh start. Instead, it is permeated by profoundly operative conceptual models which Hobbes derives from his natural cosmology and which he considers legitimately, even imperatively, applicable to political theory.

In consonance with his unidimensional cosmology, moreover, Hobbes conceives man's inertial passions as moving within a single emotional plane. Just as the heterogeneous panoply of substances found in the classical cosmos are conflated by Hobbes into the single substance of 'Body,' the varied forms of human emotion are conflated by him into a unidimensional continuum of 'appetite' and 'aversion.' 'All the passions,' says Hobbes, 'consist of appetite and aversion, except pure pleasure and pain, which are a certain function of good or evil.'[29] And appetite and aversion are not different types of motion, but simply poles of the same plane; they differ only as positive and negative, as attraction and repulsion.

All the variations in human emotion are poured into a single stratum. For Hobbes, affection, passion, pleasure, and love are equivalents: 'So that pleasure, love, and appetite, which is also called desire, are divers names for divers considerations of the same thing.'[30] And elsewhere Hobbes asserts the identity of love and lust: 'the name "lust" is used where it is condemned; otherwise it is called by the general word "love": for the passion is one and the same indefinite desire of different sex, as natural as hunger.'[31]

This conflation of all emotions into 'appetite' is a rather

radical and limiting conception of human motivation. However, it does follow quite logically from the destruction of the teleological order and rationality in nature. Classical thinkers had conceptions of appetite, too, such as Plato's notion of the appetitive part of the soul and Augustine's notion of concupiscence. But for Plato and Augustine the appetites were a distinct and limited class of human emotions. They were not to be confused with *eros* or *amor Dei*, which were the passionate, affective component of man's orientation toward the *logos*. With the obliteration of nature's *logos*, however, the ontological basis of the distinction in human psychology between love and lust, between rational and irrational emotions disappears. All motions of the human mind are left ontologically, and hence evaluatively, indifferent. Whether they be seen as good or bad becomes purely a question of subjective taste: 'Every man . . . calleth that which pleaseth and is delightful to himself, good; and that evil which displeaseth him.'[32]

It is often stated that Hobbes founded the Leviathan upon will instead of reason. This characterization is quite accurate, for the mathematicization of reason left only the passions as the repository of human nature, which is the basis of any political philosophy. The real significance of this transposition, however, is not merely that it leaves the basis of the polity in the will, but *what* this will is. For in Hobbes's psychology, the will is merely a function of the inertially modeled appetite; specifically, the will is 'the last Appetite, or Aversion, immediately adhering to the action or to the omission thereof.'[33] Ultimately, then, it is a more accurate characterization, and a more revealing one, to say that Hobbes bases the order of civil society upon 'appetite.' He has completed the cycle from which Shakespeare had predicted disaster:

> Take but degree away, untie that string
> And hark, what discourd follows! Each thing meets
> In mere oppugnancy. The bounded waters
> Should lift their bosoms higher than the shores

And make a sop of all this solid globe.
Strength should be lord of imbecility,
And the rude son should strike his father dead.
Force should be right; or rather right and wrong,
Between whose endless jar justice resides,
Should lose their names, and so should justice too.
Then everything includes itself in power,
Power into will, will into appetite;
And appetite, an universal wolf,
So doubly seconded with will and power,
Must make perforce an universal prey,
And last eat up himself. [34]

It is a measure of Hobbes's optimistic estimate of the potential efficacy of artificially contrived political institutions that he denies the last link in Shakespeare's chain of consequences. Rather than 'eat up himself,' man may instead create a sovereign power to check the naturally self-destructive consequences of unbounded appetite. If this be man's hope and salvation, it is his only one, however; for human motivation can never transcend appetite for Hobbes, only contain it.

The ultimate consequence and preeminent manifestation of Hobbes's radically transformed understanding of human emotion is his total rejection of any *summum bonum*. He declares: 'But for an utmost end, in which the ancient philosophers have placed felicity, and disputed much concerning the way thereto, there is no such thing in this world, nor way to it, more than to Utopia.' [35] With this denial, Hobbes in effect pulls the linchpin from the classical cosmos; and this step, with its profound and far-ranging implications is the logical consequence of the radical transformation of the concepts of motion and nature.

The significance of this rejection, for the interpretation of both physical motion and political action, is difficult to exaggerate. The *summum bonum* in Aristotelian and Scholastic thought represented the ultimate source of order in both the physical and the political worlds. Moreover, it was the pre-eminent expression of the isomorphism between human and natural behavior in the classical cosmos. The very same model, that of eternal, uncreated, simple, rotatory motion, represented in its physical modality the ultimate source of all natural movement and in its human modality the ultimate wellspring of human action. In both of these aspects, the *summum bonum* or unmoved mover, was the *telos* of the universe, and as such the cause of its order and life.

This interpenetration of physics and psychology at the critical point of ultimate causation is reflected in the formal congruence between the patterns discerned by Aristotle in the final book of the *Physics* and in the first and last sections of the *Ethics*. In Book Eight of the *Physics*, Aristotle concluded that all motion in the universe must finally be contingent upon some primary movent, a *primum mobile* which is itself unmoved. And this unmoved mover, he argued, is properly understood as a pattern of self-sufficient, continuous, regular, eternal, rotatory motion.[36]

Precisely the same model reappears in Aristotle's discussion of the good in the *Ethics*. The *summum bonum* or highest good is depicted as the *primum mobile* or unmoved mover of human action. The good is 'that at which all things aim'; and the chief good is that 'which we desire for its own sake.'[37] Like the unmoved mover of physical motion, the *summum bonum* is the final goal of human action, a self-sufficient and continuous activity desired for its own intrinsic worth. It is 'something final,' 'always desirable in itself and never for the sake of something else.'[38] It is 'the most continuous' and 'the most self-sufficient' form of activity.[39] On the basis of these criteria, which are exactly the same criteria which define the unmoved mover, Aristotle concluded that the highest good was the activity of rational contemplation. In its pure form man can only approximate it, he felt, but the divine can and does embody it. 'Therefore, the activity of God, which surpasses all others in blessedness, must be contemplative; and of human activities, therefore, that which is most akin to this must be most of the nature of happiness.'[40]

The whole conception of the *summum bonum*, then, was a direct function of the Aristotelian theory of motion. The *summum bonum* was, in effect, the unmoved mover of human behavior, the psychological incarnation of the *primum mobile*. And both the *summum bonum* and the unmoved mover were expressible in the same symbolic paradigm: the image of eternal, self-sufficient, rotatory motion. This symbolic form, in turn, was both the preeminent formal expression and the ultimate foundation of the closed and finite Aristotelian cosmos.

It is, therefore, only logical for Hobbes to reject the conception of the *summum bonum*, for it is the expression in the realm of psychology of a theory of motion which he has discarded. The new model of inertia removes the need for the unmoved mover in the realm of physics, and within the Aristotelian format of isomorphism between physics and psychology (which, we have argued, Hobbes tacitly accepts) it simultaneously removes the need for postulating a *summum bonum* in order to interpret human action. Hobbes is merely following out the logical implications within the formal framework of the Aristotelian cosmological paradigm of his radically transformed idea of motion when he declares that 'the Felicity of this life, consisteth not in the repose of a mind satisfied. For there is no such *Finis ultimus*, (utmost ayme) nor *Summum Bonum*, (greatest Good,) as is spoken of in the Books of the old Morall Philosophers.'[41] Felicity is not repose, for nothing is really 'at rest' in the classical sense in Hobbes's universe. Instead, happiness is itself a form of endless, linear motion, 'a continuall progresse of the desire, from one object to another, . . . a perpetuall and restlesse desire of Power after power, that ceaseth only in Death.'[42]

In short, the new concept of inertia, carried to its full logical conclusion in the setting of an integrated cosmological paradigm that takes the nature of motion as its foundation, breaks open the eternal closed circle which symbolized the classical cosmos.

The symbol of the new, infinite, inertial universe is instead the endless horizontal line. Physically, linear nonfinite motion replaces circular eternal motion; and in the human realm the transformation is formally identical. The eternal circular motion of fulfillment and contemplation is broken open and becomes the linear motion of endless striving. Hobbes's fundamental psychological model is a human equivalent of the law of inertia.

Hobbes gives his conception of human action as endless striving its symbolic expression in his image of life as a race. It is essential to this image, moreover, as Hobbes quite clearly sees, that this race be seen as having no particular direction, and indeed no finish line at all; the only aim of the competitors is to be in the forefront of the perpetual chase.

> The comparison of the life of man to a race, though it hold not in every part, yet it holdeth so well for this our purpose, that we may thereby both see and remember almost all the passions before mentioned. But this race we must suppose to have no other goal, nor other garland, but being foremost, and in it:
>
> > To endeavour, is appetite . . .
> > To consider them behind, is glory . . .
> > To consider them before, is humility . . .
> > To lose ground with looking back, vain glory . . .
> > To be holden, hatred . . .
> > To turn back, repentance . . .
> > To be in breath, hope . . .
> > To be weary . . . , despair . . .
> > To endeavor to overtake the next, emulation . . .
> > To supplant or overthrow, envy . . .
> > Continually to be out-gone is misery.
> > Continually to out-go the next before, is felicity.
> > And to forsake the course, is to die.[43]

It would be difficult for anyone to improve upon the classic simplicity and power of this symbolic characterization of human life. At the very outset of the modern era, Hobbes has produced the model of the 'rat race,' and he has done so within the context of a world view which provides it with a profound cosmological foundation. There are two significant corollaries of this model of human behavior, moreover, which are worthy of note: the universalization of anxiety and the relativization of political ends.

An irremediable anxiety, first, is the overriding subjective attribute of the man caught up in the paradigmatic race. His life is one of ultimate and endless striving, without any *telos* to fulfill his quest. He must run, but he has no resting place for his goal. While in one sense it is accurate to say, as Eric Voegelin has, that the seventeenth century destroys the tension that characterized the Aristotelian cosmos—the tension of the dialectic between potential and actual—in another sense it universalizes tension; for what is destroyed is not the striving, but the *telos* which made the strife resolvable. In human terms, then, the proximate anxiety of the finite human organism generated from its not-yet-fulfilled condition turns into the ultimate and unresolvable anxiety of the racer who is condemned to run continually after a nonexistent fullfillment. The modern Sisyphus pushes his boulder across an endless plain.

Second, the image of the race embodies the relativization of political ends in Hobbes. That is, since there remains no absolute goal of human and political life, that which remains is simply the wholly relative goal of being ahead of the other. Politics becomes a zero-sum game in which one man's success involves another man's failure, one man's power another man's impotence, one man's glory another man's shame. There is here no common good or community, but only individual competition for scarce or mutually unattainable goods.

All life, Hobbes says, is a quest of 'power after power,' and man's felicity consists of the continual attainment and exercise of power. But the very definition of power is given in relative terms. 'Power simply is no more but the *excess* of the power of one above that of another: for equal powers opposed, destroy one another.'[44] Power is a form of dominion, rather than simply a form of absolute strength. For man naturally loves dominion over others,[45] and the strengths of two men will clash rather than augment one another. Power is that which is left over, the resultant which is produced by a parallelogram of conflicting forces.

Moreover, without a structuring and limiting *telos* to govern it, power becomes autonomous. It becomes an end in itself, rather than a means to final fulfillment. Or, to put it slightly differently, the 'contentment in proceeding' which power permits is itself the only kind of fulfillment there is left in Hobbes's inertial psychology of motivation. As a consequence of becoming an end in itself, power feeds upon itself insatiably, having no objective other than still more power. Hobbes calls once more upon the model of physical motion to characterize this pattern of insatiability: 'For the nature of Power, is in this point, like to Fame, increasing as it proceeds; or like the motion of heavy bodies, which the further they go make still the more haste.'[46] Formally, this pattern of the endless quest for power after power recalls Plato's conception of the soul dominated by a master passion and foreshadows Marx's comments about the insatiably accumulative drive of capitalist man. Both resemblances are more then fortuitous.

The case of glory, upon which Hobbes places considerable emphasis, especially in his earlier works, provides a further excellent and significant instance of this relativization of political ends. All men, though some to a more immoderate degree, love glory, which is 'joy, arising from imagination of a man's own power and ability.'[47] However, glory, like the power whose imagining is its source, is a relative phenomenon. 'If all men have it no man hath it, for it consists in comparison and precellence.'[48] And since 'all society is either for gain or for glory,'[49] further substantiation is given to the overall Hobbesian depiction of politics as a zero-sum game.[50]

In sum, Hobbes's vision of the human passions and their manner of operation is profoundly shaped by his basic paradigm of motion. The means by which this structuring impact takes place is not so much substantive or deductive, which would be logically impermissible, but formal and analogical. The basic model of motion easily penetrates the conception of e-motion. Moreover, the model of motion shapes the conceptualizing of human behavior through the intermediary conception of nature, as well; for on the one hand motion is the key to the understanding of nature and on the other hand passion ('naturall passion') is one modality of the uniform operation of homogeneous nature. This pattern of analogical penetration, moreover, merely replicates the formal pattern found in Aristotle, who also conceptualized human behavior as one species of a universal pattern of movement.

Although Hobbes's analogical reasoning follows the pattern set by Aristotle, the concrete view of human behavior which results from the substantively radical transformation in the key conception of motion is far different from the classical view. The natural passions which govern men, being inertial, make human society an arena of colliding power drives. Bereft of any natural end or fulfillment, the fundamental human passion for power is infinite and insatiable; 'like the motion of heavy bodies,' the further it goes it makes 'still the more haste.'[51] In its boundlessness and disorderliness, passion is but another expression, though a critical one, of the boundlessness and disorderliness of nature as a whole. Acting through its embodiment in the wellsprings of human action, it is ultimately nature itself that produces the zero-sum game of political life. This conclusion may be reached, Hobbes feels, by inference from the concept of nature directly, by inference from the nature of the passions, or simply from experience.[52]

The dissociative, antisocial natural passions are not in themselves sinful.[53] They nevertheless constitute a deep predicament of overwhelming practical significance. Nature, in the guise of passion, is not, as Aristotle conceived it, the inspiration to and motivating force behind the creation of political society. It is the problem rather than the solution. It places man in the miserable condition where irreconcilable and insatiable passions contend against each other, offering only the prospect of war and disaster unless they are checked.

The task of politics in the Hobbesian world, then, is preeminently the task of containment — containment of the natural forces which produce a life that is, in the famous phrase, 'solitary, poore, nasty, brutish, and short.'[54] Nature, which presents man with his political predicament, will not save him from it. It will not do so, first, because it does not possess a principle of order, and second, because it has no principle of creativity. Nature will not transform the passions into emotions which can create and sustain community. The only hope for man in facing up to his political dilemma, therefore, is to control the consequences of natural passion by an institutional force of his own creation, that is, by a work of artifice.

Natural passion, although it is the source of man's political predicament and is unable to extricate man from this predicament, nevertheless does make its contribution to man's potential political deliverance. The political containment of the dissociative force of human passion must itself be a work of artifice, but passion does provide the impetus for this enterprise. Man finds within himself one natural passion which drives him into the creation of Leviathan; and that is, as Leo Strauss has capably demonstrated, the overriding fear of violent death.

Indeed, it is necessary to Hobbes's entire political program that some feature of the human psychic economy be found to perform this motivating function. For unless some component of man's natural passion is able to provide this impetus, Hobbes's political theory could be only a counsel of despair. It is not enough, given Hobbes's naturalism, for it to be necessary that man create a sovereign to extricate himself from the calamitous situation in which nature places him; it must be possible, as well. And this possibility is contingent upon the presence of some natural human desire which can impel man to undertake the burdensome steps and to make the necessary sacrifices which are intrinsic in this creative effort. The state is itself a work of artifice, a product of man's intellect and will; but man's will is a 'worke of Nature' and the motive power behind the state must therefore be found there.

The political creations of man are not part of the human quest for the *summum bonum*, for there is no *summum bonum* in Hobbes's world. Instead they are inspired by a *summum malum*, the prospect of meeting a violent death. In the Aristotelian and Scholastic view, man acted politically because he was naturally motivated to reach his end, his *telos*. In Hobbes's view, man acts politically because he naturally wishes to avoid meeting his end. No neater expression than this could be found, perhaps, of the difference in the perception of political behavior between those who inhabited a finite universe which moved toward a fulfilling end and Hobbes, who inhabited an infinite universe which embodied a restless quest for continual motion.

Man's natural passions, Hobbes feels, embody potentially conflicting tendencies which begin to become manifest under the circumstances of social interaction. Man begins with the inherent desires for dominion and eminence. Since these passions are intrinsically unattainable without frustrating the same passions in others, however, they quickly beget bitter contention and strife among men. Contention and strife in turn produce a new specter: the possibility, even perhaps the probability in such a setting, of violent death. At this point, an even more fundamental desire, heretofore latent, comes into play. All joy, whether it consists in gain, glory, or power, presupposes life. The threat to life itself, therefore, arouses the negative expression of man's most basic desire—the drive for self-preservation, for the continuation of the 'motion of limbs.'

In Hobbes's account, then, the genetically prior *libido dominandi* dialectically generates an opposing passion which is even more fundamental—the fear of violent death. It may seem strange to suppose, in this fashion, that the ontologically prior emotion, the most basic and fundamental desire, is chronologically secondary. However, this view is well substantiated by the facts of human psychic development. Although his actions are governed in part by organic drives which are self-preservative, the child's conscious desires take life for granted; they are oriented toward gratifications of various sorts, not toward the mere continuation of life. It is only later, at a heightened level of reflexive ego-awareness and under the impact of significant examples from experience, that the individual begins to absorb the contingency of his very existence, to appreciate the fact that he will die eventually and might even meet a violent, premature end. Life is logically prior to joy, but the quest for joy antedates the quest for self-preservation in the human consciousness.

As Strauss observes, Hobbes sees man as beginning life in a kind of dream world, blissfully unaware of his most basic need. 'Absorbed in the race after the happiness of triumph, man cannot be aware of his dependence on the insignificant primary good, the preservation of life and limb; failing to recognize his bodily needs, man experiences only joys and sorrows of the mind, i.e. imaginary joys and sorrows. . . . Living in the world of his imagination, he need do nothing, in order to convince himself of his superiority to others, but simply think out his deeds for himself.'[55] Only under the impact of painful experience does the reality principle begin to make itself felt. 'He can awaken from this dream-world and come to himself only when he feels in his own person—by bodily hurt—the resistance of the real world. By *damnorum experientia* man becomes reasonable.'[56]

Hobbes's hope for the foundation of a commonwealth that can secure peace for man and save him from the destructive consequences of his passion for power and glory rests upon the belief that, to borrow Freud's terminology, the reality principle can overcome the pleasure principle. Hobbes hopes and believes that the fear of violent death is stronger than the love of eminence. Once the facts are in, the relations of cause and consequence demonstrated, there will be a hierarchy of intensity

within the human passions which parallels the logical priorities
of the ends involved. Since self-preservation is logically prior
to any enjoyment whatever, then, the passion to avoid a
violent death will override the genetically prior natural passion
for dominion. The fear of the *summum malum* is the great
pacifier, the impetus for the establishment of political order.
Having considered the nature of man in Part One of the
Leviathan, Hobbes begins Part Two, 'Of Common-wealth,'
with the following paragraph which aptly summarizes this
hopeful conviction:

> The finall Cause, End, or Designe of men, (who naturally
> love Liberty, and Dominion over others,) in the introduc-
> tion of that restraint upon themselves, (in which wee see
> them live in Common-wealths,) is the foresight of their
> own preservation, and of a more contented life thereby;
> that is to say, of getting themselves out from that miserable
> condition of Warre, which is necessarily consequent (as
> hath been shewn) to the naturall Passions of men, when
> there is no visible Power to keep them in awe, and tye them
> by feare of punishment to the performance of their
> Covenants, and observation of those Lawes of Nature set
> down in the fourteenth and fifteenth Chapters. [57]

For Hobbes, then, the foundation of the commonwealth is a
sober awareness of the nature and consequences of human
passion, conjoined with the motivating force of the *summum
malum*. The origin of political wisdom is not *eros*, in Hobbes's
view, but fear. If men are able to build a secure and lasting
society, they will do so on the basis of aversion rather than
affection. 'We must therefore resolve, that the original of all
great and lasting societies consisted not in the mutual good
will men had towards each other, but in the mutual fear they
had of each other.' [58] In fact, Hobbes sees *eros* as the problem,
not the cure; for the erotic forces in Hobbesian psychology are
purely those of the dark *eros*. The affections of man are

egocentric, exhaustively a manifestation of the Augustinian *amor sui*.[59]

On the basis of his analysis of human passion, then, Hobbes is able to complete the justification of his political program. He has answered the questions which concluded the last chapter.[60] Man, the political (chess) novice, blunders into political disaster because he is governed by the natural passions for power and glory that cannot be satisfied in society. He will succeed in saving himself from the disastrous consequences of his natural passions, however, once he recognizes the causes and consequences of his actions, because the original disaster brings to life the previously tacit passion for self-preservation. And this desire for the preservation of the 'motion of limbs,' while it is genetically secondary, is logically prior and therefore motivationally dominant once it is aroused.

Therefore, man's passions are both his curse and his potential salvation. What is needed to make man's political salvation an actuality is the 'true and certain rule of our actions'[61] which Hobbes feels he has provided. His philosophy, in his view, supplies that foresight necessary to make man's fear politically efficacious. Cognizant both of his precarious situation and of the causes of his dilemma, man will naturally move to create a sovereign power by mutual covenant. 'This is the Generation of that great Leviathan, or rather (to speake more reverently) of that Mortal God, to which wee owe under the Immortal God, our peace and defence. For by this Authoritie, given him by every particular man in the Common-Wealth, he hath the use of so much Power and Strength conferred on him, that by terror thereof, he is inabled to forme the wills of them all, to Peace at home, and mutual ayd against their enemies abroad.'[62]

NOTES

1. See Robertson, *Hobbes*; Strauss, *The Political Philosophy of Hobbes*; Taylor, 'The Ethical Doctrine of Hobbes'; and

Warrender, *The Political Philosophy of Hobbes*. The quotation from Robertson is found on pp. v–vi.

2. Strauss, *The Political Philosophy of Hobbes*, p. ix.

3. Ibid., p. xi.

4. 'Philosophy and Politics in Hobbes,' in Brown, ed., *Hobbes Studies*, p. 238.

5. Meno puts the key question as follows: 'Why, on what lines will you look, Socrates, for a thing of whose nature you know nothing at all? Pray, what sort of thing, amongst those that you know not, will you treat us to as the object of your search? Or even supposing, at the best, that you hit upon it, how will you know it is the thing you did not know?' *Meno* 80 D (Loeb translation). For an insightful commentary on the significance of this problem in Western epistemology, see Marjorie Grene, *The Knower and the Known* (New York: Basic Books, 1966), esp. Chapt. 1, 'The Legacy of the *Meno*.'

6. Fontenelle wrote, for example: 'The geometric spirit is not so exclusively bound to geometry that it could not be separated from it and applied to other fields. A work on ethics, politics, criticism, or even eloquence, other things being equal, is merely so much more beautiful and perfect if it is written in the geometric spirit.'

7. *English Works*, 1: 87–88.

8. *Personal Knowledge* (New York: Harper and Row, 1964), p. 291.

9. *The Political Philosophy of Hobbes*, pp. vi–xiv.

10. *Leviathan*, p. 9.

11. Ibid., p. 79.

12. Hobbes, *English Works*, 4: 33.

13. Ibid., 2: 8.

14. Ibid., p. 9.

15. Strauss, p. ix.

16. *English Works*, 4: 83.

17. Spinoza, *Ethics*, trans. W. H. White and rev. A. H. Stirling, Great Books Series, vol. 31 (Chicago: University of Chicago Press, 1952), p. 395.

18. Ibid.

19. See *Ethics*, 2. 3, p. 378.

20. Ibid., p. 398.

21. *Leviathan*, p. 102.

22. Ibid., The relationship of glory to power in Hobbes's thought is a complex one, partly, as F. S. McNeilly has pointed out, 'because Hobbes says different and inconsistent things.' *The Anatomy of Leviathan* (London: Macmillan, 1968), p. 137.

23. *English Works*, 4: 31.

24. Ibid., p. 33.

25. *Leviathan*, p. 177.

26. Ibid., p. 139.

27. Ibid., p. 79.

28. F. S. McNeilly has perceptively suggested that it is for this reason that Hobbes tended to reduce the consideration given to glory in his later work. McNeilly says: 'It would hardly be an exaggeration to say that in *Leviathan* Hobbes does not miss an opportunity of diminishing the importance of glory in his psychological and political arguments.' The reason for this shift of emphasis, McNeilly suggests, is that in that work Hobbes strives to adhere to a 'demonstrative and conventionalist view of method,' and the phenomenon of glory had to be downplayed since it could not 'be incorporated into a "scientific" system.' McNeilly, *The Anatomy of Leviathan*, pp. 146, 151, and 150.

29. *English Works*, 1: 409–410.

30. Ibid., 4: 32.

31. Ibid., p. 48.

32. Ibid., p. 32.

33. Hobbes, *Leviathan*, p. 48. See also *English Works*, 5: 295.

34. Shakespeare, *Troilus and Cressida*, Act 1, scene 3, lines 109–24.

35. *English Works*, 4: 33.

36. See Aristotle, *Physics*, 8. 258b, 259a, 261b, 265a, 265b.

37. Aristotle, *Ethics*, 1. 1094a.

38. Ibid., 1097a.

39. Ibid., 10: 1177a and 1177b.

40. Ibid., 1178b.

41. *Leviathan*, p. 79.

42. Ibid.

43. *English Works*, 4: 52–53.

44. Ibid., 4: 38.

45. *Leviathan*, p. 139.

46. Ibid., p. 69.

47. Ibid., p. 45. In *De Cive*, Hobbes goes so far as to claim that 'all the mind's pleasure is either glory . . . or refers to glory in the end.' (*English Works*, 2: 5.)

48. *English Works*, 2: 5.

49. Ibid.

50. F. S. McNeilly has argued that the reader must carefully distinguish between the Hobbes of the *Leviathan* and the earlier Hobbes on these questions. In the *Leviathan*, he holds, Hobbes notably diminishes his earlier emphasis upon glory and the wholly relative definition of power (See McNeilly, *The Anatomy of the Leviathan*, pp. 137–55). He further conjectures that this change came about because Hobbes gradually realized that the utterly relativistic definition of political ends were not really derived from his theoretical system. Thus, as he became clearer and more consistent in his demonstrative and conventionalist method, he moved away from his earlier position.

McNeilly acutely perceives some very real shifts of emphasis in the direction of softpedaling the essentially relativistic nature of power and glory; and I am indebted to him for this insight. However, it is arguable whether the difference between *De Cive* and *Leviathan* on this issue is quite as profound as he would lead one to believe. For even though the definitions of power and glory in the *Leviathan* deemphasize their purely relativistic nature, the logic which leads to this view is still clearly present. First, power is still defined as a form of 'eminence' or 'extraordinary Strength' (*Leviathan*, p. 69), both terms which are heavily relativistic. Moreover, man is still characterized in the *Leviathan* as 'naturally' loving 'Dominion over others' (*Leviathan*, p. 139). Hence, the political ends of any one dominion-loving individual will inevitably conflict with the intrinsically opposing ends of his fellowmen; and they find themselves once more in a zero-sum game in which one must lose for the other to reach his goal. Finally, in his treatment of the state of nature in the *Leviathan*, Hobbes still depicts gain and glory as central political goals of men and explains that it is the impossibility of universal attainment of these goals that makes the 'naturall condition' of man a miserable state of war (pp. 102–3). The same theme recurs later in the *Leviathan* where Hobbes is explaining man's lack of natural sociability. This lack, Hobbes says, is a product of the intrinsically comparative and relative nature of man's political passions: 'But man, whose Joy consisteth in comparing himselfe with other men, can relish nothing but what is eminent' (p. 142).

51. *Leviathan*, p. 69.

52. See *Leviathan*, p. 104: 'It may seem strange to some man, that has not well weighed these things; that Nature should thus dissociate, and render men apt to invade, and destroy one another: and he may therefore, not trusting to this Inference, made from the Passions, desire perhaps to have the same confirmed by Experience.'

53. 'The Desires, and other Passions of man, are in themselves no Sin' (*Leviathan*, p. 104).

54. Ibid.

55. Leo Strauss, *The Political Philosophy of Hobbes*, pp. 18–19.

56. Ibid., p. 19.

57. *Leviathan*, p. 139.

58. *English Works*, 2: 6.

59. This comparative reference represents one more reason for not taking too seriously Hobbes's protestations of Christianity. He may have been a Christian; one can never be certain of another's private beliefs. It is safe to say, however, that religion was quite irrelevant to his psychology. Considering

that religion was also irrelevant to his philosophy and had only optional bearing on his theory of obligation, one is inclined toward Richard Peters's conclusion that 'Hobbes felt passionately about religion—other peoples' religion' (*Hobbes*, p. 241). For a different view, see F. C. Hood, *The Divine Politics of Thomas Hobbes* (Oxford: Clarendon Press, 1964).

60. 'Why does man, the political (chess) novice, blunder so badly in the first place? And why will he succeed in salvaging himself once he is properly instructed in the causes and consequences of his actions?'

61. *English Works*, 1: 9.

62. *Leviathan*, p. 143.

7

Conclusion and Methodological Postscript

It has been generally recognized that the brilliant and perverse political theory which Hobbes produced marked a revolutionary departure within the tradition of political thought. What has not been generally appreciated is the systematic nature of this revolutionary departure. For the relationship between Hobbes and the regnant tradition from which he came and against which he reacted was not simply that of a major change or a sharp divergence. Hobbes's political theory was not merely different from the previously entrenched Aristotelian paradigm. It constituted instead a highly systematic transformation of the established viewpoint that paralleled and borrowed from that viewpoint even while refashioning it radically and dramatically. Contesting the substance of the established Aristotelian paradigm of natural and social reality point for point, Hobbes nevertheless tacitly adopted the basic framework and pattern of interrelationships predicated by that paradigm.

This phenomenon of reaching radical conclusions by using a new focal model in the context of an accepted tacit conceptual matrix I earlier designated as 'paradigm transformation.' This study has been intended to exhibit this pattern of systematic transformation through its form as well as through its explicit propositions. The formal carry-over from the Aristotelian model of reality into Hobbes's world view is manifested in the systematic and persistent parallelism which is present when both are given an exposition which follows the 'logic-in-use' behind them.

This largely tacit paradigm matrix shared by Hobbes and

Aristotle was a perceptual framework which structured the basic relationships conceived to obtain among the data under investigation. Both philosophers assumed that nature was an integrated whole which encompassed all immanent existence, including man. Man was the preeminent work of nature, but he was part of nature nevertheless. Epistemologically, knowledge was conceived as the power of cognition isomorphic to the natural world it sought to understand. And the potentialities and limitations of political life were irreducibly structured by the potentialities and limitations of the natural order in which it was embedded.

Moreover, both Hobbes and his illustrious theoretical predecessor and antagonist shared the assumption that the fundamentally integrated natural world was composed of two essential components: a principle of movement and a substance or substances within which movement took place. The pivotal conception for both of them was that of motion. Hobbes agreed with Aristotle that the one appropriate starting point for natural philosophy was the knowledge of what motion was all about.

Against this background, the remarkably extensive and revolutionary impact of the new concept of inertia which Galileo inspired becomes intelligible. For Hobbes, this single conceptual change opened up a whole new world—or, to put it another way, this one bold intellectual stroke had to his mind made possible for the first time an accurate understanding of the world. When the fulcrum of a giant intellectual leverage system is changed, the whole system is transformed. This is what Hobbes recognized, and the recognition elated him because it resolved old conceptual dilemmas and confusions and opened new possibilities. This radical gestalt-switch in the perception of motion posed for him the question which became the starting-point for his own philosophical explorations: 'what happens to the Aristotelian world when the focal model which governed it is rejected?' That Hobbes pursued the answer to this problem thoroughly and systematically has been, I hope, demonstrated in the preceding chapters.

Hobbes, of course, was unable to generate a complete political theory out of the new cosmological paradigm which he elaborated. In the first place, he had to import into his speculations attributes of human nature which he derived from his observations of life around him, since the new cosmological paradigm was quite devoid of human substance—it was 'non-anthropomorphistic,' as Strauss says, and therefore not an adequate foundation for a philosophy of things human. And in the second place, there is always some slippage in even the most systematic political thinker between his governing ontology and his political prescriptions. All sorts of intermediate and contingent judgments as to appropriate and effective means of attaining given ends, assessments of the practical political context, and so on, intervene between one's basic world view and his concrete political policy choices. Hobbes is no exception to this rule.

Nevertheless, the new cosmological paradigm which Hobbes articulated in response to the transformed conception of motion had a profound impact on even his political ideas by establishing the basic parameters within which they had to operate and the basic problems with which they had to deal. A world of 'rest-less' motion which had no *telos* contained restless men who had no *summum bonum*. And human psyches which were so relentlessly inertial, insatiable, presented an acute political predicament on which Hobbes centered his attention. As Hobbes saw it, dispelling the illusion of the satiable ego necessitated the recognition that untutored nature was a force for political disorder rather than, as Aristotle felt, a source of political coherence. The foundation of a stable polity, then, had to be a work of artifice rather than an expression of nature. The Leviathan was that 'artificial man' which was needed as the political *logos*; his (nominalist and artificial) utterance made the world habitable for men whose nature would have led them otherwise to collective self-destruction.

Man's political hopes, therefore, lay in the realm of artifice, in social forces and institutions of his own making. Nevertheless, unless this possibility were to be a free-floating fantasy, it had to have some foundation in the natural givens of man's existence. And while Hobbes related that he often felt quite pessimistic that his life-raft to struggling men would ever be grasped, he was not in his view indulging in purely utopian exhortation. Hobbes's artifice is like Thomas Aquinas's grace: it transcends nature, but does not (and indeed cannot) abolish it. The Leviathan stands above the chaos of the ungoverned state of nature; yet he must find his footing in it.

Again, Hobbes remained consistent with his basic cosmological paradigm, if indeed he was not positively inspired by it, when he identified this natural footing of his Leviathan. One leg of the Leviathan, to extend the metaphor, stands upon natural right and the other leg stands upon the fear of violent death. The former provides the legitimacy of Leviathan, the latter provides the possibility. These two crucial foundations of Hobbes's theory were appropriately and perceptively emphasized by Leo Strauss in his analysis of Hobbes. What Strauss seemed unable to perceive, however, perhaps because of his excessively stringent criteria of what constitutes an acceptable nexus between natural and civil philosophy, is that Hobbes's conception of natural right and his conception of human motivation are shaped to be commensurate with his general paradigm of nature. Strauss tends to depict natural right in Hobbes as an *a priori* moral presupposition and to consider his view of human motivation as the product of purely empirical observations. While Hobbes may well have had multiple inspirations for these central components of his political theory, I believe that both of them fit perfectly with his central paradigm of inertial motion. Natural right grew out of man's 'natural necessity to seek *bonum sibi*,' and the fear of violent death was the converse of man's 'natural inclination' to persevere in his motion.

In the Introduction I suggested that some of the analytical concepts put forth by Thomas Kuhn in *The Structure of Scientific*

Revolutions were useful in seeking to understand the structure of Hobbes's thought and its relationship to the Aristotelian tradition which it sought to displace. And, indeed, I have used some of the Kuhnian vocabulary throughout this study. I also suggested that certain emendations and adaptations of Kuhn's ideas were helpful in using them in the context of political theory.

This is not the proper place for a full-scale consideration of Kuhn's ideas and their adaptability to the social sciences. However, in light of the increasing interest in Kuhn by social scientists representative of several fields,[1] and in light of Kuhn's own emendations to his original expression of his ideas,[2] a few reflections on this problem are in order, especially as they relate to this specific study.

One of the central criticisms of Kuhn, relevant to our concerns here, has been that the fundamental concept in his thesis—that of the paradigm—is vague, ambiguous, and consequently difficult to put into operation.[3] The basic problem here is not so much that Kuhn gave a very vague definition of a single thing, but rather that he used the same term to refer to a whole family of interrelated things. The term paradigm is applied by Kuhn, for example, to a 'standard illustration,' a 'concrete scientific achievement,' a 'set of received beliefs,' and a 'theory,' among other things.

Margaret Masterman, in fact, in an astute analysis, has claimed to discern as many as twenty-one different senses in which the term paradigm was used in *The Structure of Scientific Revolutions*.[4] A significant number of these allegedly multiple senses of paradigm are largely semantic, however. As Masterman herself says: 'It is evident that not all of these senses of "paradigm" are inconsistent with one another: some may even be elucidations of others.'[5] Nevertheless, after all the semantic problems are dispelled, there remain some real distinctions, not merely verbal ones, to be made among the different phenomena which Kuhn lumped under the heading of paradigm.

After refining out the purely semantic multiplicity of uses of paradigm, Masterman arrives at a threefold categorization of distinguishable things, all of which Kuhn had referred to as 'paradigms' in his original work. These are: 1) 'metaphysical paradigms'—sets of basic beliefs, organizing principles behind perception, etc.; 2) 'sociological paradigms'—scientific achievements accredited by the scientific community to be used like a judicial precedent; 3) 'artefact paradigms'—actual textbook examples which are the concrete models to be emulated. It can be argued, moreover, that the second of Masterman's categories, 'sociological paradigms,' actually refers more to a significant dimension or setting for the problem of scientific revolutions than to a different type of intellectual construct on a par with the other two. Scientific communities serve as the locus of and authority behind the establishment of paradigms, but they are not themselves paradigms.

We are left with two intellectual phenomena which were placed under the single label of 'paradigm' in Kuhn's first edition of *The Structure of Scientific Revolutions*. The first of these is the constellation of basic beliefs, presuppositions, conceptual assumptions, that structure the categories and interrelationships into which the data of scientific investigation are placed—the 'metaphysical paradigm.' The other is the concrete problem solution—the 'artefact paradigm'—which is taken as a suitable model for further explorations and interpretations. And indeed, Kuhn has himself affirmed that a similar twofold distinction is useful and necessary: 'Most of those differences (in the use of the term 'paradigm,' as enumerated by Masterman) are, I now think, due to stylistic inconsistencies (e.g. Newton's Laws are sometimes a paradigm, sometimes parts of a paradigm, and sometimes paradigmatic), and they can be eliminated with relative ease. But, with that editorial work done, two very different usages of the term would remain, and they require separation.'[6]

Kuhn's distinction, which he then elaborates, goes basically as follows. The first sense of 'paradigm' refers to a whole complex of deeply engrained beliefs and perceptions shared by a scientific community. This is the paradigm as 'disciplinary matrix.'[7] The second sense of 'paradigm' refers to one of the key constituent components of this disciplinary matrix, namely, to the 'concrete problem-solutions' that serve as 'shared examples' for members of a given scientific community. These 'exemplars,' Kuhn contends, constitute the central and most novel aspect of his thesis; and they are the component of the disciplinary matrix for which the term paradigm is most appropriate philologically. (The other constituent components of the disciplinary matrix, Kuhn says, are 'symbolical generalizations,' 'shared values,' and what he had referred to in the first edition as the 'metaphysical parts of paradigms.') The two senses of 'paradigm,' then, in Kuhn's revised formulation, are related as part to whole. The exemplar (paradigm 2) is a centrally important element of the disciplinary matrix (paradigm 1).

There is, then, considerable overlap, but some slippage as well, among the distinctions made by Masterman, those made by Kuhn himself, and those which were made in the Introduction to this volume. Like Kuhn in his self-revision, I suggested that a paradigm might best be conceived as a complex whole, which contained several constituent elements. When the thesis of this study refers to the 'transformation of a cosmological paradigm,' therefore, it is this complex whole paradigm which is referred to. Essentially, this is what Kuhn now chooses to label the 'disciplinary matrix,' and it bears resemblance to the notion of *Weltanschauung* or 'world-hypothesis.'[8]

For purposes of analysis, I then suggested that it was possible to distinguish at least two functionally related components of this full-scale paradigm. The first of these was a kind of bare-bones formal perceptual skeleton which served at a very simple and fundamental level to provide the framework for the more concrete substantive components of the paradigm. This framework was designated the 'tacit matrix' of the paradigm, signifying both its essential cognitive function and the usual mode of

o

its functioning. The coincidental choice of the same term, matrix, by both Kuhn and myself is perhaps unfortunate, since we are not using it with the same referent. For Kuhn, the matrix refers to the complex whole paradigm, whereas I use the term to refer to one of the constituent elements of the whole. Moreover, none of the constituent elements of the full-scale paradigm which Kuhn delineates is quite identical with what I had in mind. This lack of correspondence need not, I think, be a cause of great concern nor an indication that one of us is wrong; it simply indicates that it may be useful to break down the constituents of paradigms differently in areas which have different subject-matter.

The other analytically distinct component of the overall paradigm which I identified in the context of this study was designated the 'focal model.' I suggested, as reflected in the formal parallelism but substantive divergence in the exposition of Aristotelian and Hobbesian thought, that Hobbes had adopted the matrix of the Aristotelian paradigm but radically changed its content. The key to this change lay, it was suggested further, in Hobbes's adoption of a new 'focal model,' namely, the Galilean model of motion. Here my concept of the focal model has a very close correspondence to one of Kuhn's concepts in his breakdown of the constituent elements of his 'disciplinary matrix.' By 'focal model' I intended to convey something basically the same as what Kuhn calls an 'exemplar': the concrete puzzle-solution which serves as the analogical source of more extensive inquiry or of a more extended theory. This notion also corresponds quite closely to Masterman's 'artefact paradigms.'

There are, then, and there will continue to be, some conceptual vagueness and semantic confusion in the Kuhnian vocabulary. Some commentators have suggested that these problems raise grave doubts about the wisdom of trying to use this vocabulary in the social sciences.[9] Two appropriate rejoinders may be entered, however, against this counsel of discouragement. First, it is questionable whether these problems are insuperable. It is not at all impossible progressively to sort out the various meanings of the actual terms, to refine them, and to indicate the nature of their interrelationship. The preceding few paragraphs, indeed, constitute one example of this process of conceptual refinement and clarification, which Kuhn and others have already begun and which will undoubtedly continue. And second, the demand for absolute conceptual clarity in the early stages of the development of an analytical frame of reference is based on a misunderstanding of the nature of scientific advance. Conceptual clarity must come, but in due time. The meaning of a word, as Wittgenstein has admonished us, is its use; it follows that the uses of a concept or a 'language-game' must be explored before its meaning can be established. In the beginning of its deployment, a scientific concept generally is and must be open-ended. Premature closure in the name of clarity is both impossible and self-defeating. Abraham Kaplan, drawing upon the support of Freud, has stated the case succinctly:

> In short, the process of specifying meaning is a part of the process of inquiry itself. . . . For the closure that strict definition consists in is not a precondition of scientific inquiry but its culmination. . . . I do not think that Freud was merely rationalizing the shortcomings of his own semantic patterns in making explicit this methodological precept: 'We have often heard it maintained that sciences should be built up on clear and sharply defined basic concepts. In actual fact no science, not even the most exact, begins with such definitions. . . . It is only after more searching investigation of the field in question that we are able to formulate with increased clarity the scientific concepts underlying it, and progressively so to modify these concepts that they become widely applicable and at the same time consistent logically.'[10]

The genuinely relevant demands to levy against a family of

ideas in their early stages is not for definitive clarity but for insight and fruitfulness. When measured by these criteria, the framework which Kuhn has developed seems to me to come out rather well. 'Insight' and 'fruitfulness' are not, of course, subject to quantification, so each must make his own evaluation.

Perhaps the primary virtue of using the paradigm concept and its attendant ideas lies in their capacity to operationalize the essential findings of gestalt psychology in the context of epistemology. As Michael Polanyi noted at the outset of *Personal Knowledge*, 'scientists have run away from the philosophic implications of gestalt.'[11] Similarly, most interpretation of political theory proceeds in a very piecemeal fashion, dealing with ideas about the state, or authority, or obligation as though they were autonomous concepts which could be treated in serial fashion, isolated from the other aspects of the theory. Perhaps this form of analysis has its uses. And perhaps in the case of some theorists this is all that can be done. However, most really powerful political theories, 'epic' theories as Wolin calls them, attain their stature precisely because of their capacity to integrate these varied components into a coherent vision of the political world.

As Kuhn reminds us:

Neither scientists nor laymen learn to see the world piecemeal or item by item. . . . The Copernicans who denied its traditional title 'planet' to the sun were not only learning what 'planet' meant or what the sun was. Instead, they were changing the meaning of 'planet' so that it could continue to make useful distinctions in a world where all celestial bodies, not just the sun, were seen differently from the way they had been seen before. The same point could be made about any of our earlier examples. To see oxygen instead of dephlogisticated air, the condenser instead of the Leyden jar, or the pendulum instead of constrained fall, was only one part of an integrated shift in the scientists' vision of a great many related chemical, electrical, or dynamical phenomena. Paradigms determine large areas of experience at the same time.[12]

The same basic point, I think, needs to be made in relation to political theory. A political theory is not, except derivatively, a set of propositions. It is instead an integrated vision of the political world — the structure of its components, the relationship of these components one to another, and the relationship of this whole to its larger context. Hobbes did not simply differ with Aristotle on certain political issues; he actually saw politics in a whole different way than did Aristotle. The strength of Kuhn's concepts is that they are appropriate for the analysis of integrated perceptual gestalts of this sort.

For similar reasons, moreover, the vocabulary of 'paradigm,' 'crisis,' 'anomaly,' and so on, can illuminate the dynamics of change and development within political theory. There does exist in the process of theory construction, both in the 'hard' sciences and in political science, a kind of dynamic logic of discovery, which is not really accounted for by Aristotle's account of formal logic, by Mill's or Bacon's accounts of induction, or by Hempel's account of 'hypothetico-deduction.' Kuhn's concepts, in contrast, do capture some of this dynamic, perhaps because they are grounded in an appreciation of the complexities and ambiguities of perception. To understand a given datum as an anomaly or a given intellectual achievement as an exemplar is to see at the same time the impetus to and the source of other theoretical problems or constructs which follow logically. In the context of this study, for example, perceiving Galileo's model of motion as a new examplar which overcame certain anomalies in the Aristotelian paradigm simultaneously enables one to perceive the paths by which Hobbes was drawn to some of the conclusions he reached.

Kuhn's emphasis upon the functions of 'exemplars' may also prove helpful in the context of political theory. This aspect of Kuhn's framework, which he now considers to be the most novel part of his book,[13] explains the power that specific concrete examples may attain in the formulation of theory. While Kuhn tends to describe these exemplars in the context of natural science as solutions of particular problems or puzzles, it is possible to broaden the reference of this concept somewhat in the context of political theory. For the political theorist, a particularly striking historical event, political act, or political actor often seems to perform the perceptually catalytic functions described by Kuhn. For Plato, for example, the confrontation of Athens and Socrates delineated in the *Apology* provided the essential perception of order juxtaposed against disorder that structured his more systematic political reflections. And for Hegel, as well as for Burke, the French Revolution provided a specific concrete case which precipitated and governed the structure of his philosophy.[14]

It might be suggested, then, that one essential part of understanding the structure and logic of a particular political theory might be the identification and elucidation of the key examples which function as paradigms for the theorist's vision. This kind of investigation, moreover, might prove especially helpful in comparative analysis. For example, as I have suggested elsewhere,[15] the contrast between Hobbes and Enlightenment liberalism poses an interesting problem: both conceived themselves to be articulating the political implications of the scientific revolution, but they reached radically different conclusions. While there are many causes of this apparent paradox, part of the problem may be resolved by an appreciation of the functions of exemplar paradigms. For while Hobbes took Galileo's solution of the problem of motion as his exemplar of nature, the Enlightenment liberals took Newton's solution of the problem of gravitational force as revelatory of the activity of nature. A world conceived *sub specie* gravitation is obviously a very different place than a world conceived *sub specie* inertia. The former world is a much more orderly and coherent one, and the predicament of political man in such a world is not so dire. Instead of having to extricate himself from the chaos of 'meer nature,' as Hobbes put it, he can instead simply follow Diderot's exhortation to 'return to nature' and all else will be given unto him. Says Diderot: 'Return to Nature from which you have fled; she will console you and dispel all those fears which now oppress you. Submit to nature, to humanity, and to yourself again; and you will find flowers strewn all along the pathway of your life.'[16]

If one sees nature in this light, as a principle of order and coherence, like the force of gravitation, he is not likely to be on the road to Leviathan. If anything, he is more likely to be on the road to laissez-faire. Indeed, Adam Smith wrote with unabashed admiration of the Newtonian system[17] and perceived the world as an 'immense machine' which God had 'contrived and conducted . . . so at all times to produce the greatest possible quantity of happiness.'[18] On these premises, so far from being forced to ingenious political artifice in order to escape the manifest disorder of nature, political man is counseled to avoid resort to artifices, which will interfere with the course of nature's benevolent designs: 'Projectors disturb nature in the course of her operations on human affairs, and it requires no more than to leave her alone and give her fair play in the pursuit of her ends that she may establish her own designs. . . . Little else is required to carry a state to the highest degree of affluence from the lowest barbarism but peace, easy taxes, and a tolerable administration of justice; all the rest being brought about by the natural course of things.'[19] Smith, Diderot, and others such as Priestley and Condorcet, did not deduce their political precepts straight from Newtonian mechanics, of course. But Kuhn's insight into the functions of exemplar paradigms in theory construction helps us to see the analogical force which Newton's law of gravitation had for them. Moreover, some of their striking contrasts with that other interpreter of the political implications of the new science, Hobbes, are clarified at the same time.

It is too early to render any final judgment on the entirety of Kuhn's provocative analysis of scientific inquiry. For example, it is not yet clear whether Kuhn's model will be able to provide a satisfactory account of the process of 'verification,' of the reasons for scientific 'progress,' or of the rational grounds for choosing one paradigm over another.[20] Later clarification may dispel some of the criticisms which have been leveled against Kuhn on these issues. Or it may be that Kuhn's framework cannot provide an acceptable answer to some of these problems. Nevertheless, it is not too early, I believe, for an appreciation of the genuine heuristic value of some of Kuhn's central insights and suggestions.

In the case of this study, the application of Kuhn's categories was largely *ex post facto*. The basic thesis and most of its elaboration had already been completed before I first encountered *The Structure of Scientific Revolutions*. Kuhn's ideas, therefore, did not contribute to the original formulation of the study; and the book could undoubtedly have been written without it. Nevertheless, Kuhn's model contributed materially to the final product in several ways. In the first place, Kuhn's insights served to consolidate and to clarify some of the basic analytical contentions of the work. In doing so, moreover, they provided an appropriate vehicle of exposition—a language which has been disseminated widely enough that its use may facilitate communication. And finally, Kuhn's model served as an essential heuristic tool in expanding the scope of the argument: the crystallization of the central pattern of 'paradigm transformation' led, for example, to the extension of the argument which is embodied in Chapter Five.

One final word about the world of Thomas Hobbes: in some ways we still inhabit it. Hobbes's specifically political recommendations have hardly been widely embraced, but some of the fundamental aspects of his paradigm persist into contemporary ideas and problems. Hobbes limits the rational faculties of man to the process of 'computation'; and we debate whether human knowing involves any powers not possessed by 'thinking machines.' Hobbes depicts the psyche as a conglomerate of positive and negative motions, appetites and aversions; and twentieth-century psychological behaviorism builds its psyche out of 'stimulus-response' arcs.[21] Hobbes argues that 'whatsoever is the object of any man's appetite or desire, that is it, which he for his part calleth good';[22] and we discuss the 'emotive theory of ethics,' which holds all ethical statements to be an expression of merely subjective preference. Hobbes dissolves the *telos* of human striving and thereby makes anxiety an irremediable condition; and contemporary man worries aloud about his 'age of anxiety.' Hobbes says that life is like a race that has 'no other goal, nor other garland, but being foremost';[23] and we ponder how we might escape the 'rat race.'

It is probably true, as E. A. Burtt says, that 'it has been worth the metaphysical barbarism of a few centuries to possess modern science.'[24] However, there are more than purely speculative dangers inherent in the persistence of this 'metaphysical barbarism': it may contribute to political barbarism. For, as Michael Polanyi has warned, there are certain political implications which follow from a Hobbesian cosmology that displaces man. 'Then law is no more than what the courts will decide, art but an emollient of nerves, morality but a convention, tradition but an inertia, God but a psychological necessity. Then man dominates a world in which he himself does not exist. For with his obligations he has lost his voice and his hope, and been left meaningless to himself.'[25]

The logic of the seventeenth century's cosmos may lead to Leviathan, as Hobbes suggests. It may be implicated in behaviorist utopias of social engineering.[26] It might lead, as some have argued, to a politics of nihilism and violence.[27] Or men may be able simply to suspend the logic of their fundamental beliefs and govern their political actions by a common sense which they somehow know to be wiser than their theory.[28]

In any case, the logical political implications of the Hobbesian seventeenth-century world view are not exceptionally inviting. One would prefer some other choice than that among the *Leviathan*, the *Possessed*, or *Walden Two*.

The difficulty is that a prevailing paradigm is never, as

Kuhn explains, utterly discarded until an equally comprehensive paradigm is discovered which can function in its stead.[29] And, despite some strikingly important additions and alterations to it, the 'characteristic scientific philosophy which closed the seventeenth century . . . is still reigning.'[30]

We may be witnessing, however, the gradual emergence of a new cosmological paradigm—one that would restore man to a place in the world.[31] Whitehead thought so; and others have made a similar claim.[32] The sense of impending crisis in the regnant paradigm seems already to be present, in any case. As Kuhn says, 'today research in parts of philosophy, psychology, linguistics, and even art history, all converge to suggest that the traditional paradigm is somehow askew.'[33]

If this indeed be the case, then it is especially important that we understand the contours and the foundations of the seventeenth-century world view. For the development of a new paradigm can proceed with clarity only if the structure of the paradigm which it seeks to displace is clearly perceived. As twentieth-century men, therefore, we have practical as well as purely theoretical reasons for the kind of inquiry embodied in this study. Just as Thomas Hobbes clearly understood the world of Aristotle, we must understand the world of Thomas Hobbes.

NOTES

1. See for example, Sheldon S. Wolin, 'Paradigms and Political Theories,' in *Politics and Experience*, ed. King and Parekh (London: Cambridge University Press, 1968), pp. 125–52; Robert Friedrichs, *A Sociology of Sociology* (New York: The Free Press, 1970); J. G. A. Pocock, *Politics, Language, and Time* (New York: Atheneum, 1971); A. W. Coats, 'Is There a "Structure of Scientific Revolution" in Economics?' *Kyklos* 22 (1969): 289–95; Martin Bronfenbrenner, 'The "Structure of Revolutions" in Economic Thought,' *History of Political Economy* 3 (1971): 136–51.

2. See the 'Postscript' to the second edition of *Structure of Scientific Revolution* (Chicago: University of Chicago Press, 1970), and 'Reflections on My Critics' in *Criticism and the Growth of Knowledge*, ed. Imre Lakatos and Alan Musgrave (London: Cambridge University Press, 1970).

3. See for example, George J. Stigler, 'Does Economics Have a Useful Past?' *History of Political Economy* 1 (1969): 217–30. 'My main quarrel with Kuhn is over his failure to specify the nature of a paradigm in sufficient detail that his central thesis can be tested empirically' (p. 225).

4. See Margaret Masterman, 'The Nature of a Paradigm,' in Lakatos and Musgrave, *Criticism and the Growth of Knowledge*, pp. 59–89.

5. Ibid., p. 65.

6. Kuhn, 'Postscript,' pp. 181–82.

7. Kuhn says that he uses the term ' "disciplinary" because it refers to the common possession of the practitioners of a particular discipline; "matrix" because it is composed of ordered elements of various sorts, each requiring further specification.' Ibid., p. 182.

8. See Stephen C. Pepper, *World Hypotheses* (Berkeley: University of California Press, 1942).

9. See for example, George Stigler, 'Does Economics Have a Useful Past?' *History of Political Economy* 1 (1969): 217–30.

10. Abraham Kaplan, *The Conduct of Inquiry* (San Francisco: Chandler Publishing Co., 1964), pp. 77–78.

11. Polanyi, *Personal Knowledge*, p. xii.

12. Kuhn, *The Structure of Scientific Revolutions*, pp. 127–28.

13. See 'Postscript,' p. 187.

14. At least, such is the interpretation of Eric Voegelin in 'On Hegel—A Study in Sorcery,' a paper delivered before the graduate seminar in the history of the social sciences at Duke University, Spring 1971. 'The impact of the Revolution,' Voegelin argues, 'was indeed the experience that fundamentally formed Hegel's existence' (p. 10).

15. 'The Politics of Inertia and Gravitation: The Function

of Exemplar Paradigms in Social Thought,' to be published in *Polity*, Spring, 1973.

16. Quoted by Ernst Cassirer, *The Philosophy of the Enlightenment*, trans. C. A. Koelln and James P. Pettigrove (Boston: Beacon Press, 1955), p. 135.

17. See the concluding section of his 'Essay on the History of Astronomy': 'Newton's principles, it must be acknowledged, have a degree of firmness and solidity that we should in vain look for in any other system.' *The Essays of Adam Smith* (London: Alex Murray and Co., 1872), p. 384.

18. Ibid., p. 210.

19. From a lecture Smith gave in 1749, cited by Jacob Viner, 'Adam Smith and Laissez Faire,' in *Adam Smith, 1776–1926* (Chicago: University of Chicago Press, 1928), p. 119.

20. See the criticisms by Dudley Shapere, 'The Structure of Scientific Revolutions,' *The Philosophical Review* 73 (1964): 383–94, and 'The Paradigm Concept,' *Science* 172 (1971): 706–9; Israel Scheffler, *Science and Subjectivity* (Indianapolis, Ind., Bobbs-Merrill, 1967).

21. For a characterization of Hobbes as the original behaviorist, see Floyd W. Matson, *The Broken Image* (Garden City, N.Y.: Doubleday, 1966), chaps. 1 and 2.

22. Hobbes, *Leviathan*, p. 41.

23. Hobbes, *English Works*, 4: 52.

24. *The Metaphysical Foundations of Modern Science* (Garden City, N.Y.: Doubleday, 1954), pp. 305–6.

25. *Personal Knowledge* (New York: Harper and Row, 1964), p. 380.

26. Hobbes tells us at the outset of the *Leviathan* that man is to be conceived as both 'the matter' and 'the artificer' of the commonwealth. In a similar fashion, B. F. Skinner admonishes us because we have not followed this logic to its conclusion: 'We have not yet seen what man can make of man.' *Beyond Freedom and Dignity* (New York: Alfred Knopf, 1972), p. 215. The latent, critical question which must be put to those like Skinner is, 'does that mean what you can make of me or

what I can make of you?' Or, in Hobbes's terms, who is to be the artificer and who the matter?

27. See Michael Polanyi, *Beyond Nihilism* (London: Cambridge University Press, 1960), and *The Logic of Liberty* (London: Routledge and Kegan Paul, 1951).

28. The model of this 'suspension of logic' is David Hume, returning to his game of backgammon after having reached an impasse of utter skepticism in his philosophical speculations. See *Beyond Nihilism*, p. 18.

29. 'The decision to reject one paradigm is always simultaneously the decision to accept another.' *Structure of Scientific Revolutions*, p. 77.

30. Alfred North Whitehead, *Science and the Modern World* (New York: New American Library, 1959), p. 55.

31. In the seventeenth century, man 'lost his place in the world.' Alexander Koyre, *From the Closed World to the Infinite Universe* (Baltimore, Ind.; Johns Hopkins Press, 1957), p. 4.

32. See for example, R. G. Collingwood, *The Idea of Nature* (New York: Oxford University Press, 1960); E. A. Burtt, *The Metaphysical Foundations of Modern Science*; Marjorie Grene, *The Knower and the Known* (New York: Basic Books, 1966); Michael Polanyi, *Personal Knowledge*; and Milio Capek, *The Philosophical Impact of Contemporary Physics* (Princeton, N.J.: Van Nostrand, 1961).

33. *The Structure of Scientific Revolutions*, p. 120. See also my recent argument on the corresponding situation in political science in *The Dilemma of Contemporary Political Theory* (New York: Dunellen Co., 1972).

Index